Sarah Williams is a very experienced writer, with more than eighty titles published. She founded and runs the increasingly popular Thriller School in the UK and in the US, where readers, writers, scientists and crime fighters come together to explore all the different facets of crime-fiction writing. She is a member of the Society of Authors and of the Crime Writers' Association.

HOW TO WRITE CRIME FICTION

Sarah Williams

A HOW TO BOOK

ROBINSON

ROBINSON

First published in Great Britain in 2015 by Robinson

Copyright © Sarah Williams, 2015

The moral right of the author has been asserted.

A CIP catalogue record for this book
is available from the British Library.

ISBN 978-1-84528-569-2 (paperback)
ISBN: 978-1-84528-590-6 (ebook)

Typeset by Basement Press, Glaisdale
Printed and bound in Great Britain by CPI Group (UK) Ltd., Croydon, CR0 4YY

Robinson
is an imprint of
Constable & Robinson Ltd
100 Victoria Embankment
London EC4Y 0DY

An Hachette UK Company
www.hachette.co.uk

www.constablerobinson.com

How To Books are published by Constable & Robinson, a part of Little Brown Book Group. We welcome proposals from authors who have first-hand experience of their subjects. Please set out the aims of your book, its target market and its suggested contents in an email to Nikki.Read@howtobooks.co.uk

For J

Acknowledgements

The author is grateful for permission to include extracts from the following works:

MURDER FORTISSIMO by Nicola Slade 2011. Extract printed by permission of Robert Hale.

THE BURNING WIRE by Jeffery Deaver 2010. Extract printed by permission of Hodder & Stoughton Ltd.

NOTHING TO LOSE by Lee Child 2008. Extract printed by permission of the Random House Group Ltd.

PICTURE HER DEAD by Lin Anderson 2011. Extract printed by permission of Hodder & Stoughton Ltd.

THE EXECUTIONER by Chris Carter 2010. Extract printed by permission of Simon & Schuster UK Ltd.

SAINTS OF THE SHADOW BIBLE by Ian Rankin 2013 John Rebus Ltd. Extract printed by permission of the Orion Publishing Group Ltd.

RED MIST by Patricia Cornwell 2011 CEI Enterprises, Inc. Extract printed by permission of the Penguin Group.

THE BRASS VERDICT by Michael Connelly 2008 Hieronymus, Inc. Extract printed by permission of the Orion Publishing Group Ltd.

THE HIDDEN MAN by Charles Cumming 2003. Extract printed by permission of HarperCollins Publishers.

THE RIVERS OF LONDON by Ben Aaronovitch 2011. Extract printed by permission of the Orion Publishing Group Ltd.

THE SILVER PIGS by Lindsey Davis 1989. Extract printed by permission of the Random House Group Ltd.

BEASTLY THINGS by Donna Leon 2012 Donna Leon and Diogenes Verlag AG, Zurich. Extract printed by permission of the Random House Group Ltd.

EVIL RELATIONS: THE MAN WHO BORE WITNESS AGAINST THE MOORS MURDERERS by David Smith with Carol Ann Lee 2011. Published by Mainstream. Reprinted by permission of The Random House Group Ltd.

IN COLD BLOOD by Truman Capote 1966. Extract printed by permission of the Random House Group Ltd.

LAST EXIT TO FUENGIROLA by David Hewson 2014. First appeared in the Crime Writers' Association anthology *Deadly Pleasures*. Extract printed by permission of Severn House Publishers Ltd.

CONTENTS

INTRODUCTION

It's probably fair to say right now that this isn't a recipe book or a manual. Writing isn't like cooking a meal or putting together a chest of drawers (though it may well have elements of both). Writing is a very strange mixture of the personal – your ideas, your voice, your take on things – and the public – the readers, their expectations, their interpretation. This book is aimed at helping you do two things, and to do them well – to identify the kind of crime-fiction novel or short story you'd like to write, and to explore some of the key elements of that kind of crime fiction, so that you can be clear about what you need to do to meet your readers' expectations. It's not that you can't deviate from the template (in fact, it would hardly be possible to write something worth reading without doing so); it is rather that you need to be aware of what the 'rules' are, so that, when you break them, you do so consciously, for effect, rather than by mistake in a way that disappoints or frustrates your readers.

In order to help you do this, there are exercises throughout the book in which you can play with different ideas, different ways of saying things, different ways of putting events and characters together.

What works best for you?

There are fundamentally three different ways in which you can approach this book. None of them excludes the others – it's more a question of what will work best for you.

The first approach is simply to read through the book from beginning to end, to get an overview of the landscape of crime-fiction writing, and of all the highly varied kinds of writing and plot-building available.

The second approach is to read the book through, doing all the exercises as you go along. This is an approach that is particularly helpful and appealing to new writers looking to hone their craft. There are few better ways of becoming a better writer than to experiment with writing in different ways, using different vocabulary, sentence structures, tones of voice and imagery.

In order to make this as practically useful for you as possible, each chapter focuses on an excerpt from the work of a specific, highly successful contemporary author writing in that genre, and each chapter provides, as well as a number of 'building' exercises, one Core Exercise, each of which focuses on one particular aspect of crime-fiction writing. Taken together these form the foundations of a complete crime-fiction writing course.

Finally, if you are already clear and confident about the kind of crime fiction you want to write, then, if you work through the chapter on that genre in detail, it will give you pointers and reminders about the kind of things you will need to do or bear in mind if you are to write in that genre successfully and satisfy your readers' expectations.

It's worth pointing out, though, even if you are only interested in one particular genre, all the exercises throughout the book will be helpful as you hone your craft. The writing techniques typical of one genre can often prove extremely useful when writing in another genre and, of course, there is often a great deal of overlap between genres.

Examples and technical terms

As mentioned, each chapter opens by looking at a short passage by a contemporary writer who is an expert in the genre – a difficult choice on every occasion because there are so many superb crime writers publishing today. Each author, and each passage, has been chosen not only because the writers are great practitioners of their craft, but also because the particular passage selected demonstrates important aspects of the kind of writing under discussion. At the end of the book you will find a glossary of technical terms. These have been used as little as possible, but, equally, these terms have been developed as useful analytical and explanatory tools so it is helpful for the writer to know them. In order not to interrupt the flow of the reader's concentration, each term is marked in **bold** on its first use so that, if you are unfamiliar with it or unsure of its meaning, you can nip to the back of the book, have a quick glance at the glossary and then proceed.

One last thing – I have sought to be thorough and informative about the vast and ever-changing landscape of crime fiction. I will, inevitably, have missed things out, or categorized writers or styles of writing in ways that others would query. Much of the categorization of these different kinds of fiction is down to interpretation and emphasis. At the end of the day, what is important is that you take from each chapter what is useful to you, in order to explore, hone and develop your own writing, and find your own voice. Enjoy your writing.

CHAPTER 1
THE DIFFERENT KINDS OF CRIME FICTION

The idea of enjoying reading books about people being burgled, bullied, tormented, tortured and killed is, to say the least, an odd one. Yet crime fiction is almost as old as the novel form itself, and it certainly wasn't long before it developed as a separate and distinctive genre – a genre that is more popular today than ever before.

Why does crime fiction exist?

There are all sorts of answers to that question but, as this is a book for writers, I will stick here to the answer that seems to me to be most practically useful to a writer. Crime fiction provides a way for the writer, and thus for the reader, to explore extreme situations in which questions of morality – what it is to be good or bad, what it is to behave well or ill, constructively or destructively – are brought to the fore, without either the writer or the reader actually having to expose themselves to those situations in reality.

The categories of crime fiction

That's a very broad-brush attempt at a definition. Perhaps it's more useful to look at what happens in the different kinds of crime fiction, not so much in terms of the **plots** as in terms of how the world of the book is left when the **story** ends and where the book takes the reader. It is possible to see the different kinds of crime-fiction story as falling into one of three broad categories:

1. Putting the world to rights
2. Taking you behind the scenes
3. Taking you away from the world you know

Before going on to look in detail at each of the separate genres of crime fiction, as we shall be doing throughout the rest of this book, let us just take a moment to look at what each of these three broad categories consists of, and what implications that has for the writer.

To some extent, all fiction, perhaps all literature, can be seen as an exercise in putting the world to rights, even if it's only in terms of showing just how singularly not right the world is, in the writer's view. But crime fiction, more than any other kind of literature, is concerned with confronting a transgression, identifying a transgressor and, in one way or another, restoring the moral order. This is true of all crime fiction, but it is perhaps pre-eminently the case with 'cosies'.

The cosy

The world of the cosy is a world in which moral and social order are the expected norm. It depicts a circumscribed world, usually a village; one totally trustworthy character, who is both highly intelligent and slightly underrated by many of those around her (and it usually is a 'her'); and a violent crime, the interest of which lies not in the violence but in the puzzle surrounding it. The moral order is restored by the solving of the puzzle, the apprehension of the perpetrator and the restoration of the world of the book to its customary equanimity.

The consulting detective

Something similar is the case in 'consulting detective' crime stories, such as those involving Edgar Allan Poe's Auguste Dupin, or Sir Arthur Conan Doyle's Sherlock Holmes. There are important differences, though. First of all, the world of the book is much more flexible and fluid, both socially and geographically. Equally, the consulting detective (most often male) is usually more of a maverick, standing slightly at odds to the society that he serves and whose ills he addresses.

Hardboiled crime fiction

The 'hardboiled detective', such as Raymond Chandler's Philip Marlowe, is a development of the figure of the consulting detective, but darker, even more of a maverick, no longer necessarily a gentleman, yet with a totally reliable, if wry, sense of right and wrong.

In all of these three kinds of crime fiction, the writer must establish their central figures as having two fundamental characteristics: they need to be clever and they need to be good. The reader has to be able to trust them, both in terms of the moral order and in terms of their ability to sort through the chaos and confusion of the crime or crimes, and put things right again.

Noirs and thrillers

Things get slightly less cut and dried with the last two genres in this section: the 'noir' and the 'thriller'. In each of these the central **protagonist** on whom the reader relies to solve the mystery and put the world to rights is not necessarily an entirely nice, pleasant or reliable person. The hero or heroine is usually tormented, tarnished and tousled, and the world in which they move is confused, dark and often brutal.

A continuum of crime fiction

In a slightly simplistic but nonetheless generally accurate way, one could see these five different kinds of crime fiction as operating along a continuum like this:

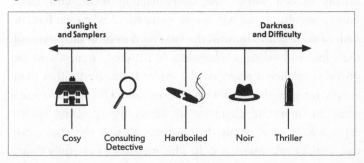

7

As we will see when looking at each of these genres in detail, the position on the continuum you choose for your protagonist and for the world of your story will have important repercussions for the choices you will be making as a writer – plot, narrative voice, language, imagery and all the rest.

There is, of course, as we have already seen, no cut-and-dried division between the different genres of crime fiction – they necessarily link and overlap, and there are frequently very fuzzy boundaries between one and another. Nonetheless, there is an important difference in emphasis between the next four kinds of crime-fiction story we will be looking at here and those that we have just been discussing.

Specialists in fighting crime

Police procedurals, forensic crime fiction, courtroom crime fiction and spy stories all depend for their interest and effectiveness on the unfamiliar details of the different worlds to which they introduce the reader. What this means for the writer is easy enough to state but sometimes very hard to achieve: the details must be accurate or, at the very least, entirely consistent, convincing and intriguing.

Expert knowledge and research are key here, and, almost as important, a light touch. The writer must perform a judicious balancing act between letting the reader into this specialist and usually hidden world, and overwhelming them with facts. Fundamentally, as we will see in more detail when we look at each of these genres in turn, the facts need to be at the service of the plot, and where explanation is required, it needs to be provided in such a way that the reader is involved rather than simply hit over the head with information. This is why there's often an 'innocent' character to whom the specialist has to explain X, Y or Z about their subject, so that the reader can receive the explanation as well. This needs to be carefully done, though, if the specialist is not to come across as tedious and patronizing, and the reader is not going to be tempted to leave them to it and go and make a cup of tea.

Police procedurals, courtroom crime fiction and spy fiction have a lot in common in terms of the way in which the reader is introduced to and kept within the unfamiliar world of police work and spycraft. Frequently, as we will see, this is done by using 'insider language' in such a way that the meaning is clear to the reader, while giving them a sense of being a member of the inside team themselves. For instance, to pick just one example more or less at random, in Michael Connelly's Harry Bosch series, there is frequent mention of the Murder Book. Fundamentally, this is simply the ring binder in which every action and every piece of evidence is recorded throughout the investigation of a homicide case in the United States. The slightly creepy name used with easy familiarity, and the fact that the name is often employed in a casual and offhand way, gives the reader a sense of inclusion within the inner world of the homicide detective.

Similarly, in spy fiction, use of 'technical' terms such as 'asset' or 'wet work' immediately places the reader within the world of espionage, with all its extraordinary vocabulary of dissimulation and pretence.

All the different kinds of forensic crime fiction work in a comparable but slightly different way – the forensic scientist is an expert, a specialist, whose extraordinary skill we are invited to learn about as if we are looking over their shoulder. While the reader may be one of the team, as it were, in police procedurals and spy fiction, in forensic crime fiction the reader's position is much more that of the admiring outsider or, at the very most, an apprentice.

Transporting the reader to different times, different places

In terms of crime fiction, there is a range of different ways of using different times, different places, different experiences of reality into which the reader can delve. You can take your reader into an identifiable historical past, you can introduce them to an alternative version of the reality they feel they know, or you can whisk them away to a different part of the globe, where the geographical and cultural setting is distinctive and imaginatively engaging.

Crime fiction set in past times has become increasingly popular of late, and it is easy to see why. It is history at street level, so to speak, with the pleasure of being taken inside the places, the culture, the thinking of peoples we have probably just brushed past in our schooldays. If you are interested in a particular historical figure, or a particular historical period, then exploring that person or that period through the medium of a crime-fiction novel can be profoundly rewarding. The judicious mixture of minutely researched historical fact with the freedom of fictional invention enables writer and reader alike to inhabit a world both familiar and unknown, while the addition of a crime or crimes immediately raises questions about what, morally and personally, we have in common with peoples in past times, and what things we see radically differently.

Killing a partner in a jealous rage may seem understandable, if undesirable, in any culture at any time – but beating a child? In our current Western culture this may be seen as a criminal offence punishable by imprisonment; in another time it would perhaps simply have been viewed as good parenting. Historical crime fiction sets up a series of mirrors in which we can catch fascinating glimpses of other times, times that have helped to shape our own. Simultaneously, we see our own culture, assumptions and behaviours reflected back at us from odd angles. And all with characters to get to know and puzzles to solve . . .

Paranormal crime fiction is another genre that is becoming increasingly popular, and which has a power all of its own. To write effective paranormal crime fiction is extraordinarily difficult, though – not more difficult than other kinds of crime fiction, but with different, and perhaps more extreme, temptations and traps for the writer. This is something we will look at in more detail later on, but it's something of which to be aware from the start if this is the kind of writing to which you are drawn.

Fundamentally, the power of the paranormal rests on our belief in two worlds simultaneously – the world with which we are familiar, which we regard on an everyday basis as the 'real world', and the world created and evoked by the writer – a world that needs to be entirely as consistent and convincing as the world we take for granted. It is hardly surprising, when our experience of the 'real world' has changed so radically over the past twenty to twenty-five years, with the invention and application of information technology, the internet and the World Wide Web, that our interest in and acceptance of the paranormal should have grown so greatly.

Every day, the vast majority of us are making use of technologies of which we have little or no understanding – saying 'boot up the server' might just as well be saying 'abracadabra' for all we understand of the mechanisms behind the action described by the phrase (although, of course, the language of technology is seen as being much more 'respectable' in our science-based age). So, to some extent, the writer of paranormal crime fiction today has a head start over anyone attempting the same genre a hundred years ago. Your readers' willingness to accept apparently outlandish occurrences as being perfectly possible has already been extraordinarily expanded by the incomprehensible but incontrovertible genius of the likes of Albert Einstein and Sir Tim Berners-Lee. Having said that, though, the writer of paranormal crime fiction does have two challenges that need to be addressed with clarity and deftness: making the world of the paranormal internally consistent, and explaining its particularities without being either boring or patronizing. As with forensic thrillers, the use of an 'innocent' to whom things need to be explained is often handy here.

The last of the three crime fiction genres in this section is also the most recently developed, and that is the crime story set in an exotic location. Not that crime fiction hasn't always to some extent played with the glamour or seediness of foreign parts – think Ian Fleming or Eric Ambler among writers of previous generations. But now there is a vast range of crime fiction that deliberately draws on the foreign setting, the exotic location, as a crucial element in how the story actually works.

However, I would draw a distinction between that and crime fiction set in, say, Sweden or Italy, written by a Swede or an Italian and translated into English. Here, the location was not exotic to the writer, however unfamiliar it might appear to their English-language reader. The exotic-location crime-fiction stories we are concerned with here are rather those written in English, by English-speakers, and set in countries where English is not the first language. In these books, much as in historical crime fiction, the reader has the sense of having an intimate insight into a world that is normally hidden and inaccessible. The particular balancing act for writers of this kind of crime story is to enable the reader to be taken inside this unfamiliar world, while still maintaining its strangeness and avoiding even a whiff of cultural tourism or ex-colonial condescension. Again, we shall look at ways of achieving this in greater detail a little further on in this book.

The real thing: writing true crime

The world of true-crime and fictionalized true-crime writing is primarily concerned with the subject matter and how you handle it. At first sight, this would seem to be the simplest of all kinds of crime writing – all you need are the facts, and then you set them out in a well-arranged fashion for your reader, rather like bananas on a market stall. However, as with the notional stall-keeper and his bananas, the writer of true-crime stories needs to be carefully selective about what goes out on the stall, and how it is displayed.

To put it at its baldest, most of what happens in the unfolding and solution of a crime or a series of crimes, however horrific, is fundamentally very boring, and so the writer needs to select from among the plethora of facts just those that their readers will find interesting – and this immediately brings the writer up against a singularly difficult set of choices.

There are two things that, I feel it would be fair to say, most readers find interesting about true crime: *what* actually happened and *why* it happened. If you like, the mechanics and the motivation of murder. Describing the mechanics of murder, rather like the mechanics of sex, easily moves from the factual to the unintentionally absurd, and from detached description to lubricious pornography. In fact, to be honest, it is probably not the simple fact of a man using a saw in the bedroom of his home that readers will find interesting, but the fact of a man using a saw in the bedroom of his home to dismember someone he has drugged and murdered. It is the shock of the transgressive act that engages the reader.

The writer of true-crime stories, therefore, has to tread a delicate path between saying what actually happened and dwelling inappropriately on the messier or more macabre aspects of the murderer's actions. Simply telling the story is usually not enough – which is why fictionalized true crime seems so much more rewarding a route, for reader and writer alike, though it, too, has traps set for the unwary.

Keeping it short

The short story is a very demanding literary genre with distinctive requirements. The form is particularly well suited to crime fiction, where the economy and concentration of the format can be exploited to great effect, particularly if your taste turns to the unexpected ending. Writing short stories is a very different craft from writing novels and requires very particular skills, as we'll see.

How everything fits together

Section and Chapter	Section Focus
Part 1: Putting the World to Rights	Plot, character and voice
Chapter 2: The Cosy	
Chapter 3: The Consulting Detective	
Chapter 4: The Hardboiled Crime Novel	
Chapter 5: The Noir	
Chapter 6: The Thriller	
Part 2: Taking You Behind the Scenes	Language and detail
Chapter 7: The Police Procedural	
Chapter 8: The Forensic	
Chapter 9: Legal Fiction	
Chapter 10: The Spy Novel	
Part 3: Taking You Away From the World You Know	Place and dialogue
Chapter 11: The Paranormal	
Chapter 12: The Historical	
Chapter 13: Exotic Locations	
Part 4: The Long, The Short and the Rather Tall Story	Focus and selection
Chapter 14: True Crime	
Chapter 15: Fictionalised True Crime	
Chapter 16: The Short Story	

Chapter Focus	Author in the Spotlight	Core Exercise
Structure and timelines	Nicola Slade	Event Grid
Protagonist/antagonist	Jeffery Deaver	Building Character
Narrative voice and POV	Lee Child	Who Knows What?
Plot points	Lin Anderson	Seeding Information
Pace and sentence structure	Chris Carter	Taking the Temperature of the Book
Specialist vocabulary	Ian Rankin	Deciding What Matters
Technical detail	Patricia Cornwell	Showing and Telling 1: Telling
Insider view	Michael Connolly	Positioning the Reader
Implication and explanation	Charles Cumming	Showing and Telling 2: Showing
Evoking place	Ben Aaronovitch	Metaphor and Simile
Dialogue and detail	Lindsey Davis	Giving Voice
Place as character	Donna Leon	Creating Place
Telling details	David Smith	Telling Details
Selection	Truman Capote	Shaping the Narrative
Shining a narrow beam	David Hewson	Staying in Focus

PART 1:
PUTTING THE WORLD TO RIGHTS

TECHNICAL FOCUS:
PLOT, CHARACTER AND VOICE

CHAPTER 2
THE COSY

Author in the Spotlight: Nicola Slade
Chapter Focus: Structure and timelines

In this passage from Nicola Slade's *Murder Fortissimo*, which appears a little way into the book, we are being brought more closely into the world of the convalescent home in which the events will take place, and are given some intimate insights into the character and attitudes of the main protagonist, Harriet Quigley. As you read through the passage, keep an eye out for all the information you are given about Harriet. How do you see her, and how do you think she sees herself?

Harriet Quigley shifted to a more comfortable position and congratulated herself on her strategy. No way, she thought, would she allow friends and neighbours to ferret her out, and the retreat had worked well enough as a cover story. She felt a pang of guilt about her cousin Sam. Maybe I should have told him, she admitted to herself, but I can't help being such a wimp about hospitals and I certainly didn't want anyone else to know; hence the sphinx-like silence at that wretched dinner party.

No, Sam was squeamish too and since his wife's death he was out of touch with 'female troubles'. Harriet winced at the memory of the consultant as he briskly informed her 'it's better out than in, nothing to worry about but you'll be more comfortable, start running marathons? Take up trampolining?' He had spoken only the truth however. The day or two in the smoothly efficient private hospital, now to be followed by a gentle recuperation at Firstone Grange, looked set to do the trick; none of the lying around for weeks that Harriet remembered from her mother's experience.

Her terror of hospitals had been, well, *lulled* was the word, though not diminished. Although she still felt very tired, Firstone Grange, she considered, was doing her proud so far; pleasant staff, delightful room with its own bathroom, delicious food. So far it was living up to its promise, and so it should considering the cost, but . . . she cast a discreet glance round the room. I'm not so sure about some of the other inmates though. Residents, guests even, she corrected herself hastily, not inmates. Matron certainly wouldn't like that word.

From *Murder Fortissimo* by Nicola Slade

The cosy is perhaps the most tightly organized of all the forms of crime fiction at which we will be looking. There are a number of reasons for this but the main one is that the cosy is supremely dependent on plot, or, perhaps more accurately, on there being a puzzle to be solved. The essential elements of a cosy are threefold: a small cast of characters in a relatively confined location; a crime (usually a murder), the method and motives of the perpetrator of which appear baffling; and a clever, quiet observer who gradually assembles the clues and solves the mystery.

Sorting out the plot

The primary decision for you as a writer, then, once you have an idea of your main protagonists, is to work out what happens and why it is mysterious. Plotting a cosy is one of the most rigorous of all forms of fiction writing because the plot has to hang together, all the clues have to be available for the reader (but positioned in such a way that they don't see them) and the dénouement has to have the effect of making the reader go, 'Oh, of course!' and then flip back through the story to see, in retrospect, just where all the clues were laid out if only they had been able to notice them . . . It is a bit like writing a story, composing a crossword and putting together a Sudoku grid all at the same time.

Before looking in detail at the passage from Nicola Slade, perhaps one of the foremost contemporary practitioners of the form, it is worth taking a look at the plot.

Structuring your book

I have found it helpful, from a practical point of view, to draw a distinction between three different elements in fiction writing that are sometimes used almost interchangeably. The differences between them, though, are important, and very useful when planning and playing with the structure of your book.

The term 'the world of the book' is often bandied about and generally taken to mean the reality conjured up by the author and entered into by the reader. On this occasion, though, I'd like to be slightly more literal and suggest that each book is like a world in an almost geological sense. Without labouring it too far (and without claiming any but the most superficial understanding of the actual geological processes), I would like to suggest that there is a useful comparison to be drawn between the structure of a book and the structure of the earth.

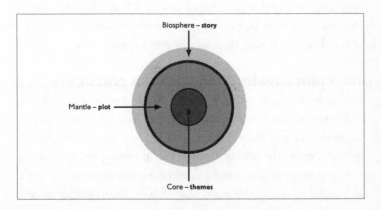

At the centre of the book lie the **themes**, unimaginably hot and dense, and accessible only through observing the outer layers of plot and story. The plot holds everything together, but is occasionally disrupted, distorted, shifted and changed by forces from below, while the story is, as it were, the grass, the mountains, the trees and rivers, the oceans, clouds, creatures and creations, and all the complexity of stuff that makes up the world we recognize and inhabit.

What does this mean for you as a writer? It means that you need to be very alert to the different natures of these three elements and to how you want them to interact – because, of course, you are in control of every part of your world and can shape it as you will.

The interplay between these three elements is something to which we will come back at different points throughout this book, since theme, plot and story each take on a different weight and significance depending on what kind of crime fiction writing you are engaged in. Here we are concentrating on cosies, and it is time now to look in detail at how a cosy is put together and how you might write yours.

The crucial thing about a cosy is the plot – everything focuses on that. The setting is confined, the characters few: it is the slow unfolding of events that matters most. And that, of course, means that your plot must be carefully, consciously constructed, with each of the characters having their specific part to play.

How plot construction works in practice

Let us look briefly at how Nicola Slade positions the central character in *Murder Fortissimo* in the passage quoted at the beginning of this chapter, and then see how that positioning is going to guide the reader through the unfolding of the plot.

This passage occurs about a third of the way through the book, at a point where all the main players have been established and they have all gradually been drawn together to be focused in the one geographical area, Firstone Grange, a short-term private residential care home for the wealthy infirm. (It is interesting to see how so many cosies have followed the historical changes in large country houses over the last hundred years or so, from family residences with weekend parties to privately owned health facilities of one kind or another – each providing a confined space with a small group of characters.)

We have already encountered Harriet Quigley at the opening of the book, as a guest at 'that wretched dinner party', and she has been established as an intelligent and reliable observer. She had a slightly mysterious motivation for a fortnight's stay at Firstone Grange, which is here explained as being a combination of 'female troubles' and 'being a wimp about hospitals'. Nicola Slade has thus engineered a thoughtful, intelligent, reliable, discreet and more or less able-bodied observer to be a witness to the events at the Grange as they unfold, and to be the reader's guide through to the solution of the crime. Harriet's slightly ironic but essentially sympathetic attitude is signalled by the last few sentences of the passage quoted above.

Creating a canny observer

As we have seen, a reliable, intelligent, canny observer who can unravel the events and lead the reader safely to the solution is an essential element of a cosy. It is worth spending some time thinking through who that character might be, what their background is, and how and why they become involved in solving whatever mystery you are going to use to intrigue your readers. (Also worth bearing in mind is that publishers like crime-fiction series – so if your 'problem-solver' can have a sufficiently substantial backstory and good enough reasons to be an observer of more than one odd event, to be unfolded over two, three or even more books, then you will be well-placed when looking to sell your work.) Answering the questions below will help you start the process of creating your observer, your problem-solver, the character on whom your readers will depend:

1. Name
2. Background
3. Where they live
4. The kind of life they lead (give yourself lots of leeway for detail here – descriptions, note forms, bullet points – whatever works best for you)
5. How they appear to others
6. How they appear to themselves
7. What makes them good at problem-solving
8. How they get involved (in this story specifically)

Add as many other elements as you need to give yourself a very solid central character – about whom you will know much more than your readers will ever need to know.

Choosing your crime

But what of the core element to be considered in a cosy – the question of the crime? Why is it a mystery, and how is it to be hidden from and then revealed to the reader? The plotting must be meticulous – there is probably no more demanding group of readers in terms of plots, clues and coherence than those devoted to cosies. They are going to be on the lookout for diversions, distractions, the sensation of dust thrown in the eyes and the scent of red herrings in the nose. Of course, you have two major advantages over your bloodhound readers – you are completely in control of what they discover, glimpse or guess, and you actually know all the answers. But, in order to lead them through the maze, bumping them up against dead ends and blind corners, only to bring them out into the clear sunlight of the solution at the end, you need to create very clear maps, notes or grids for yourself of what happens when, who does what to whom, and who knows which bit of the puzzle and how it is revealed. This doesn't mean, of course, that new ideas and better twists and turns will not occur to you when you start writing, but it does mean that every alteration to your original plan will need to be checked against your notes, maps or grids to make sure that you haven't thrown the unfolding of the plot out of balance.

Organizing the elements

So what should these maps, notes or grids be about and how should you organize them? I would suggest five general areas with which to start – you may find you need fewer, or more, or that an altogether different way of planning works better for you, but try these for a start, see where they take you, and then make the modifications you need to enable the plotting and storytelling work for you – and for your readers.

1. What happens

The first area involves establishing a list or grid of characters who are going to be taking part in your story, the second needs you to draw a map of the place or places where your crime occurs, and the third sets up the chronology of what happens, from the opening of the book through to the solution of the crime at the end. Before tackling any of these, though, there is one crucial piece of planning which you need to lock down – who does what to whom, where, and why. This doesn't have to be very detailed – it can be much more along the lines of playing Cluedo (known as Clue in the United States): 'It was Colonel Mustard in the library with the lead pipe', but with the addition of victim and motive – and, of course, your crime doesn't have to be a murder . . .

CORE EXERCISE: EVENT GRID

Complete the table

Villain	Victim	Crime	Location	Motive

2. Who's involved

Now draw up a list of all the central characters in your story, again in a fairly spare form: what you need to work out is who they are, where they function within the geography of the book (scullery maids tend to be stuck in the scullery unless you give them a reason to get out – an affair with the milkman, picking herbs for cook in the kitchen garden . . .), what they do (if anything) in terms of the plot, what they know about the crime and how we, the readers, learn about what they know. Your list for a character could look something like this:

1. Name: Cecilia Jones
2. Age: Beyond middle age, not yet elderly

3. Likes/dislikes: Enjoys order, quiet, regularity – the church flower rota, roast lamb on Sundays . . .

4. Where they work/what they do: Vicar's wife

5. Where she's usually to be found: Vicarage and vicarage garden

6. Role in the plot: Discovers a single large leather glove under a rosebush

7. How we know what she knows: Tells her husband over dinner

You can, of course, add as many different headings to your character lists as you feel you need – the point is to enable you to feel that you know everybody and the role they're going to play in your story.

3. Where it all takes place

Having established in your mind a rough outline of what happens, who is involved, what they know and how their knowledge is revealed to the reader, it's time to lock down where your events take place. Whether this is a real place or an imaginary setting, you need to have a map of the physical place in which your characters are functioning so that you can make sure that Ethel really could see the murderer's hat as she was hanging out the washing in next-door's garden. Every place has to be clear in your head, and you need to know how each place relates to the others, how it is possible to move between them and how long it would take. It's no good providing an alibi for one of your characters that requires them to be able to have lunch in London and afternoon tea in Adelaide on the same day, or even to be in the cellar and the attic of a house simultaneously . . . You may find you need to draw a number of maps, depending on what you have happening and how much ground your characters cover.

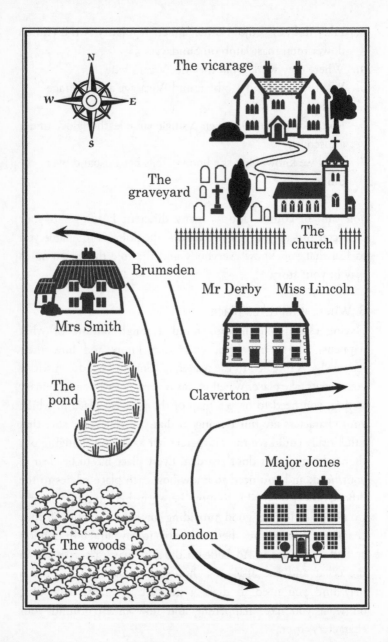

4. What happens when

Finally, and linked to both the characters involved and the physical layout of the location, comes the chronology of events – a timeline. For this, it's often useful to work backwards from the end, and, as it were, reverse engineer the timing of the events based on what you need to have happened by the final scene of the book.

Again, how you do this depends very much on how your mind works and what you find are the best tools for organizing your ideas. It's often useful to create a top-down flowchart, a bit like a fault tree analysis, so that you can work out what must have happened prior to the end result, in a logical sequence.

Careful and detailed planning at this stage pays huge dividends later, both in terms of the way in which you can comfortably develop the plot when you're writing and also in the satisfaction that your readers will get from your book. Readers of cosies tend to be eagle-eyed problem-solvers, and if they see how everything fits together at the end of the book and that your whole plot was logically structured, they will be a great deal happier.

5. Laying false trails

There is one last element that it's worth planning out, which is how the clues and the false trails are going to be deployed through the book so that the solution is not obvious as the reader works through the story but is seen to be inevitable once they come to the end and look back. This is a bit like designing a three-dimensional chessboard, but it can be broken down into a series of elements that you can use as reference points as you write. Draw up a table with five columns and fill them in so that you have a list of:

a. What the significant clues are
b. What the confusing elements are (the misdirection, in magicians' terms)
c. Who discovers which clue

d. How they discover that clue
e. To whom that clue is revealed

One visual aid that may be useful is to see the clues as being part of an enormous pizza which has got broken up and scattered about. Your characters come across a slice here, a slice there, sometimes a single olive, sometimes a bunch of anchovies – and your problem-solver reassembles the entire pizza at the end of the book. Following this gastronomic **simile**, elements of misdirection could be other bits and pieces (slices of ham, chunks of pineapple . . .), which could belong on a pizza, but don't belong on this one . . .

All these together provide you with the skeleton of the plot and how the different elements hang together. Now it's over to you to use these as guidelines, and to write your story, checking constantly that you're not asking the characters to be in two places at once or to have witnessed an event that has yet to occur . . .

CHAPTER 3
THE CONSULTING DETECTIVE

Author in the spotlight: Jeffery Deaver
Chapter Focus: Protagonist/antagonist

Lincoln Rhyme is a consulting detective and, in the passage below, we see him apparently triumphant over his arch-**antagonist**, the Watchmaker. Jeffery Deaver spells out quite clearly here the similarities and differences between Rhyme and the Watchmaker. What are they, and what in the passage suggests that this relationship is far from over?

Rhyme now realised that Richard Logan, sitting cuffed and shackled in a chair between two uniformed patrolmen, was speaking to him. In a cool, eerily analytical voice, the killer repeated, 'A setup? All fake. You knew all along.'

'I knew.' Rhyme regarded him carefully. Though he'd confirmed the name Richard Logan, it was impossible to think of him as that. To Rhyme he would always be the Watchmaker. The face was different, yes, after the plastic surgery, but the eyes were those of the same man who'd proved every bit as smart as Rhyme himself. Smarter even, on occasion. And unbridled by the trivia of law and conscience.

The shackles were sturdy and the cuffs tight but Lon Sellitto sat nearby anyway, keeping an eye on the man, as if the cop thought that Logan was using his considerable mental prowess to plan an escape.

But Rhyme believed not. The prisoner's darting eyes had taken in the room and the other officers and had concluded that there was nothing to be gained by resisting.

'So,' Logan said evenly, 'how did you do it?' He seemed genuinely curious.

As Sachs and Cooper logged and bagged the new evidence, Rhyme, with no small ego himself, was pleased to indulge him.

[…]

[The detective] nodded and they headed for the door. The Watchmaker turned back, saying coyly, 'I'll see you again, Lincoln.'

'I know you will. I'm looking forward to it.'

The suspect's smile was replaced by a perplexed look.

Rhyme continued, 'I'll be the expert forensic witness at your trial.'

'Maybe there. Maybe someplace else.' The man glanced at the Bréguet. 'Don't forget to keep it wound.'

And with that he was gone.

From *The Burning Wire* by Jeffery Deaver

This extract comes from very close to the end of *The Burning Wire* – Lincoln Rhyme, the consulting detective, has, through the power of his intellectual reasoning, laid a trap for and caught his arch-enemy, the Watchmaker. In the Lincoln Rhyme series, Jeffery Deaver has set up a very clever contemporary variation of the figure of the consulting detective first developed by Edgar Allan Poe and Sir Arthur Conan Doyle. Like Dupin and Holmes, Rhyme is an astonishingly clever deductive reasoner and, as with the Poe and Conan Doyle stories, all the clues are carefully arrayed for the reader (very systematically in Deaver's case, with 'evidence' and 'profile' charts laid out in the text and updated as new events occur).

Establishing intellect and ego

Deaver has ingeniously solved the problematic relationship between a consulting detective and contemporary law enforcement organizations by making Lincoln Rhyme a forensic scientist who, through a tragic accident, is now a quadriplegic. He depends on the information brought to him by law enforcement officers and other forensic specialists, but fundamentally, as he is virtually unable to leave his townhouse, he has to solve the crime through the power of his mind alone. And that, the enormous intellect, together with the enormous ego, is one of the defining characteristics of the consulting detective – they are always amazingly, breathtakingly, flamboyantly clever.

It is perhaps useful to make a distinction here between the cleverness of the protagonist of a cosy and the cleverness of the consulting detective. In the cosy, the problem-solver (as we have already noted, usually a woman) tends to be quiet and self-effacing as well as penetratingly intelligent. In the case of consulting detectives (most often men), they are, as a rule, confidently conscious of their superior intelligence – think Agatha Christie's Poirot and 'the little grey cells'.

CORE EXERCISE: BUILDING CHARACTER

We will come back to look in further detail at all that Jeffery Deaver achieves in the passage quoted at the beginning of this chapter, but it would probably be useful now for you to spend some time thinking about your own central character, their personality and the life circumstances that enable them to act as a consultant, rather than as an employee. For now, just choose two or three important characteristics of your consultant, one or two physical 'markers' (e.g. Sherlock Holmes's pipe, Poirot's moustache) and their life circumstances – are they, perhaps, retired from a law-enforcement organization or maybe they're an academic?

THE CONSULTING DETECTIVE

1. Name
2. Gender
3. Background – what they used to do
4. Life circumstances – what they do now, financial position

5. Where they live
6. Family
7. Friends
8. Helpers
9. Personality
10. Physical markers (appearance, accessories . . .)
11. Motivation – why do they do what they do?

THE IMPORTANCE OF THE ANTAGONIST

Now that you have an idea as to who your central character is, it is worthwhile looking at the character of their opponent – often an arch-enemy, like Holmes's Moriarty, against whom your consultant runs up again and again. The opponent needs to be clever, almost as clever, and sometimes even cleverer, than your main character – and to have a similar ego. If we go back to looking at the Jeffery Deaver extract, you'll see what I mean. The Watchmaker, who recurs in a number of novels, has 'proved every bit as smart as Rhyme himself. Smarter even, on occasion.' Deaver indicates that there is a special understanding between Rhyme and the Watchmaker. Rhyme has watched his thought processes and understood that the Watchmaker is not going to make a bid to escape – just then, at any rate.

The final exchange between the two of them is a typical jostling for power – Rhyme saying, more or less, 'See you in court, where I'll make sure you're put away,' and the Watchmaker responding with his own threat, 'Maybe there. Maybe someplace else.' And then Deaver has the Watchmaker have the final word – a reminder to Rhyme about the expensive watch he wears, and its link to himself – 'Don't forget to keep it wound' implies 'Keep ready, you haven't seen the last of me.' The threat is left hanging in the air as the Watchmaker leaves.

When asked about the Watchmaker in a recent interview (see www.jefferydeaver.com/novel/the-burning-wire/interview/),

Deaver was quite explicit about the importance of the antagonist:

> I think every Sherlock Holmes needs a Professor Moriarty, James Bond needs his Blofeld – it's the brilliance of the antagonists that bring out the brilliance of the heroes. In fact, I think the bad guys should be more brilliant than the good guys – otherwise, when (or if) the villains are defeated, we feel less satisfaction because our protagonists didn't have to work so hard.

So now the next thing for you to do is to draw up a few notes for your arch-villain, noting down his character, a few characteristics, and his driving motivation – it is not enough for the modern reader to have a villain who is simply bad because he enjoys being bad – there must be some driving force behind his actions, be it revenge, anger, ambition . . . So, what is it going to be for your villain?

THE OPPONENT

1. Name
2. Gender
3. Life circumstances – what they do, financial position
4. Where they live
5. Any friends, family, helpers
6. Personality
7. Driving force

Finally, you might like to draw up a chart of the similarities and contrasts between your two main characters – they are both brilliant and driven. In what other ways are they alike? In what ways are they different? Below is the start of the kind of grid you might like to develop – the longer and more detailed you make it, the easier it will be to create your characters and show how they interact when you come to write.

Characteristic	Consulting Device	Opponent
Intelligence		
Wit		
Social skills		
Moral values		
Humour		

What is the crime?

In a way, the consulting detective crime story is a bit like a cosy, but with a broader canvas and painted in more lurid colours. What this means for you is that the crime with which your protagonist is going to be faced is either extreme and outlandish or affects a larger group of people than those usually at risk in a cosy. The crime, usually, will threaten innocents as well as those directly targeted and will cover whole communities, cities, nations – sometimes even the entire globe. So your challenge is to come up with a sufficiently exotic, lurid or disturbing crime to engage the immense intellect of your protagonist – and to have been put together by the immense intellect of his antagonist. It is worth spending a little while thinking about what kind of crime this could be, how it could be carried out, who would be affected by it and how it might be discovered or foiled.

1. The crime
2. Who are the (potential) victims?
3. What does the antagonist want to achieve?
4. Why?
5. How is the crime to be carried out?
6. How is it discovered?
7. How does the consulting detective defeat his opponent?

You will also need to put together all elements of the plot, places and timeline, which we already looked at in Chapter 1. If you find it helpful, you could adapt the exercises there to your needs here so that you have a clear overview of everything that is happening, where, when and how.

Drip-feed clues or a sudden reveal?

There is one more major decision you need to make before you start to write, and that is whether you want your reader to pick up the clues as the story proceeds or whether you want your consultant to reveal the solution with a flourish at the end. Either works well with this kind of crime fiction. Fundamentally, it is a question of whether the reader has access to your protagonist's thinking as we go along or whether they are as baffled as all the lesser intellects in the story. Each has its own advantages – and its own pitfalls.

The advantage of taking your readers into the protagonist's confidence, as it were, is that it gives a pleasant sense of being part of the inner circle and of being almost, if not quite, on the same intellectual level as the very clever consultant. The disadvantage is that the tension of the unfolding story must lie elsewhere than in the unravelling of the clues – perhaps in whether a victim or victims will be saved in time, or whether the villain will actually be caught or will escape to wreak havoc another time.

The advantage of the sudden reveal, on the other hand, is the involvement that the reader feels in trying to work out the solution before the final flourish – it's something like the dance of the seven veils – you show a little, and hint at a lot . . . As with cosies, this means having the ability to structure the plot, and scatter both genuine clues and misdirection throughout the book in such a way that they give nothing away at the time, but make perfect sense at the end.

The choice is yours.

CHAPTER 4

THE HARDBOILED CRIME NOVEL

Author in the Spotlight: Lee Child
Chapter Focus: Narrative voice and point of view

In the Jack Reacher novels, Lee Child is drawing on a very old and long-established stereotype – that of the knight errant, travelling the land, righting wrongs and then moving on. But Reacher is much more than a stereotype – what do we learn about his character and attitudes from this opening passage from *Nothing to Lose*? And how do we learn it?

The line between Hope and Despair was exactly that: a line, in the road, formed where one town's blacktop finished and the other's started. Hope's highway department had used thick dark asphalt rolled smooth. Despair had a smaller municipal budget. That was clear. They had top-dressed a lumpy roadbed with hot tar and dumped grey gravel on it. Where the two surfaces met there was an inch-wide trench of no-man's-land filled with a black rubbery compound. An expansion joint. A boundary. A line. Jack Reacher stepped over it mid-stride and kept on walking. He paid it no attention at all.

But he remembered it later. Later, he was able to recall it in great detail.

Hope and Despair were both in Colorado. Reacher was in Colorado because two days previously he had been in Kansas, and Colorado was next to Kansas. He was making his way west and south. He had been in Calais, Maine, and had taken it into his head to cross the continent diagonally, all the way to San

Diego in California. Calais was the last major place in the northeast, San Diego was the last major place in the southwest. One extreme to the other. The Atlantic to the Pacific, cool and damp to hot and dry. He took buses where there were any and hitched rides where there weren't. Where he couldn't find rides, he walked. He had arrived in Hope in the front passenger seat of a bottle green Mercury Grand Marquis driven by a retired button salesman. He was on his way out of Hope on foot because that morning there had been no traffic heading west towards Despair.

He remembered that fact later, too. He wondered why he hadn't wondered why.

From *Nothing to Lose* by Lee Child

Lee Child is probably one of the most successful contemporary writers of hardboiled crime fiction and an extremely useful writer for an aspiring author to study, partly because his approach to writing is so methodical. When Granada TV was restructured in 1995, Child, who had been a presentation director, found himself being made redundant. He decided that, rather than going back into employment, he would earn his living writing fiction. Before ever setting finger to keyboard, though, he thought long and hard about the kind of books he wanted to write and about what would appeal to his readers. Thus Jack Reacher was born, an ex-military policeman in the US Army, tall, imposing and highly intelligent. It was a deliberate choice on Child's part to have Reacher completely mobile, with just a toothbrush in his pocket and access to cash when necessary (a recent concession to the changing times has been to give Reacher a credit card). Child wanted his hero to be able to move from place to place across the United States, as a kind of modern-day knight errant, righting wrongs, embracing damsels and then travelling on.

The intelligence, the physical competence and the maverick nature are all hallmarks of the hardboiled detective. The fact that

Reacher is an ex-military policeman with great respect for the military (and greatly respected by the military), and that he is rootless with neither home nor family (apart from a briefly appearing brother), gives him a greater than usual aura of toughness and independence. He is a man alone, acting as he sees best.

The nature of the hardboiled detective

These qualities, while giving the writer a lot of freedom in some respects, also call for particular skills in order to make the character credible. The independence, the physical strength, the toughness, can all be established through description and through the unfolding of the plot. Much more difficult to establish, and absolutely central to the success of the character and to the reader's commitment to the story, are the character's reliable moral compass and their intelligence. It's not enough simply to say he or she is very good and very clever – assertions alone won't cut it. The moral soundness and the intelligence have to been shown to the reader through language and action. This, as we will see in later chapters, lies at the heart of the crucial distinction between '**showing**' and '**telling**' – the good writer does both in a way that will guide but not bully the reader.

How the narrative works

If we look in detail for a moment at how Lee Child opens *Nothing to Lose*, in the passage quoted above, we can begin to see how these techniques work in practice. The first thing to notice is that Child is writing in the third person, using a **third-person narrator**, but very much from Reacher's **point of view**. This has a dual effect for the reader: we know in intimate detail what is going on in Reacher's mind – 'he remembered it later' – but we also have a kind of helicopter view from which we can see not only what is going on at that time in the narrative from Reacher's point of view, but also what happened in the past and, at least by the lightest of allusions, what was going to happen in the future. How does this affect the reader?

First of all, we are seeing the world through Reacher's eyes – and Reacher's eyes are extraordinarily observant. We are not just given a description of the road surfaces marking the boundary line between the two tiny Colorado towns of Hope and Despair – we are given an account of how the surfaces are laid, the relative costs and what implications that has in terms of the municipal budgets available to the two towns. All in the blink of an eye, as Reacher strides down the road. That is only a small portion of what is going on in this opening paragraph, but it is enough for us, as writers, to be thinking about for now. Extremely deftly, with a very light hand, Lee Child has given us a picture of the geographical location in which the story is to unfold, while at the same time letting us learn something of Reacher's knowledge, understanding and thought processes, without anywhere telling us that Reacher is observant, highly well-informed, and supremely skilled at deductive reasoning.

Secondly, the helicopter view, encompassing a knowledge of past, present and future, provides the reader with a tingle of suspense – something significant is going to happen between this moment now, when we are walking with Reacher down the road towards Despair, and the time when Reacher is looking back over the events we are about to witness. 'But he remembered it later', and 'He remembered that fact later, too', are like the suspense chords in a movie, resonant with threat.

This overarching view of the world of the book, and the implication of impending danger, has another effect on the reader as well. Child, in that opening paragraph, has brought us to identify with Reacher – we are seeing the world through his eyes, interpreting it through his mind. Then Child introduces this sense of a nebulous, unspecified threat. Inevitably, the reader becomes uneasy. We know that Reacher survives because he is able to look back on the experience, but just *what* does he survive and *how*? Because we are identifying with Reacher, we, as readers, are worried for him and for ourselves as well – to some extent, we *are* Reacher while the narrative lasts.

We have gone into this opening to *Nothing to Lose* in some detail because it highlights very effectively a number of the choices that you, as a writer of hardboiled detective fiction, will need to make.

Who is your protagonist?

The first choice to make, of course, is who is your protagonist, what is their background and what motivates them. What do they need to be to keep your reader comfortable?

I would suggest that they need to have all of the following attributes, or some variation of each of them:

1. To be employed as a detective or to have a background in law enforcement.
2. To be sufficiently skilled to be able to handle themselves in physical confrontations (this could be psychologically able to defuse the situation, skilled in the use of weapons, good at unarmed combat or simply, as with Reacher, extraordinarily fit and strong, and with a handy level of military training).
3. To be highly intelligent – though this could be a fairly hidden quality, rather than the glaring brilliance of the consulting detective.
4. To have a strong sense of morality that the reader can rely on. This is crucial: if you are going to have a protagonist who is a loner, dispensing their own view of justice, then we, as readers, need to be able to give our agreement and assent. More than any other figure, the hardboiled detective is the knight errant of contemporary fiction, on an endless quest to right wrongs and to rescue the downtrodden.

It's worth having a pause at this point to think in some detail about these aspects of your protagonist, or at least to play with possibilities.

Location, location, location

Once you've roughed out your protagonist, you need to come to some decisions about where they're to be based and how significant location is to be in your stories. As we've seen, Lee Child deliberately chose to have Jack Reacher not to have a fixed home (although one book does focus on a home he is bequeathed and the problems that poses for him). Robert Crais sets his stories in LA, Sara Paretsky has her protagonist, V. I. Warshawski, predominantly based in Chicago.

If you're going to use one fixed location as the setting for your story, and you are intending to write a series based around this protagonist and your chosen location, then it would be a good idea to choose a location where a lot of varied crimes can occur without stretching your readers' credulity. The county of Midsomer, featured in the British television series *Midsomer Murders*, has an estimated crime rate twice that of the actual crime rate of London – making the high incidence of unfortunate events in Midsomer something of a running joke among the British public.

Also, if you are going to choose a specific location to which you are going to return again and again, it is a good idea to choose a place that you know well, and with which you can easily keep up to date. Even the wonders of Google Earth are always months and sometimes years out of date.

Finally, in terms of location, you need to decide just how significant the place is to the unfolding of the story. We'll be looking at this in more detail when discussing crime fiction set in exotic locations (Chapter 13). For now, simply have a think about where would be a good place to set your stories – what would make a good backdrop for your protagonist, and what would provide a likely source of dramatic action for the plot.

1. Where does your protagonist hang out?
2. Is this where the action takes place?
3. What is your location like (urban/rural/harsh/idyllic . . .)?
4. What kinds of crimes are likely to take place there?
5. What kinds of crimes will your protagonist get involved with?

Choosing the narrative voice

Finally, you need to make a decision about the narrative voice you are going to employ and what implication that is going to have for the way your plot unfolds.

Fundamentally, there are three main choices of narrative voice for a fiction writer to pick from:

1. **The omniscient narrator**
2. **The first-person narrator**
3. **The unreliable narrator**

1. The omniscient narrator: This is the most common narrative voice used in fiction writing and it comes with all sorts of benefits for the writer. Essentially, an omniscient narrator knows everything about everybody in the story, from their taste in coffee to their most intimate thoughts and feelings. Since all the characters are the writer's own creations it is, of course, necessarily the case that the writer knows every inch of every one of them. Equally, the fact that the writer shares that knowledge with the reader means that we, as readers, have a privileged view into the internal workings of a whole range of different people as they interact. We know each of them as well, or better, than we know ourselves. This is particularly powerful when the reader holds information about the thinking and motivation of

different characters that they do not have about each other. When we know that the murderer is thinking about killing X, while we see X going blindly about their business of grocery shopping or cleaning out their closet, it gives a terrible feeling of powerless inevitability to the unfolding plot.

The central drawback of an omniscient narrator is twofold. Firstly, it's very unlike life as we experience it – we have enough difficulty making out our own thoughts, intentions, emotions and motivations. Those of other people are at best guesswork. Secondly, it has to be handled very deftly, particularly in crime fiction, if suspense is to be maintained.

The solution to this is to use a tightly focused beam of omniscience, so to speak, where we, as readers, are privy to the innermost thoughts and feelings of the central character, but share that character's inability to see into the inner life of those they encounter – a bit like real life, in fact. This is something of what Lee Child is doing in the passage quoted above, and is a very powerful and effective narrative technique for crime fiction.

2. The first-person narrator: Put simply, this is where the protagonist is presented as being the teller of the tale. This is the technique used to enormous effect by Raymond Chandler in the Philip Marlowe books. It enables the writer to establish their protagonist's character in an extraordinarily intimate way by revealing the unfolding events not just through their eyes, but also through their voice. It is a technique that has both a strength and a weakness in the narrow viewpoint from which we see the action – the protagonist, and therefore the reader, can only know what they themselves see or learn about from being told by others. This can build the suspense very effectively but it can also hamper the flow of the story – you, as the writer, have to make sure that your protagonist can plausibly obtain all the information they need to solve the problem with which they're faced.

3. The unreliable narrator: The clue is in the title – the unreliable narrator is, in every sense of the word, a very tricky character. One of the advantages of an omniscient narrator, from the reader's point of view, is that we can trust what they say – they provide the solid ground from which we view the unfolding action of the story. For instance, Jane Austen's narrators provide the reader with unquestionably the 'right' view from which to see the action. For good or ill, such a position of certainty is very rarely available in real life. The technique of the unreliable narrator is, in part, an answer to that problem, by providing a viewpoint which is much more realistic, in being partial and not necessarily accurate.

It is not a technique much used in crime fiction, simply because of the critical importance of having a moral centre to the book, a vision of good and evil, on which the reader can rely. An interesting move in the direction of having an unreliable narrator as the protagonist of a crime novel is the figure of Jeff Lindsay's Dexter, the sympathetic serial killer. Lindsay neatly sidesteps the reader's uneasiness at sympathizing with a sociopath by locating the moral centre of the book in Harry's Code – the guidance provided by Dexter's foster father, Harry Morgan, to enable him to function as a serial killer, but only of supremely bad people.

CORE EXERCISE: WHO KNOWS WHAT?

Each narrative voice has its own strengths and weaknesses. As a writer of hardboiled crime fiction, you will need to choose the voice that will best help your reader understand, identify with and trust your protagonist. Equally, each narrative voice enables you to provide different kinds of information to the reader in different ways, so your choice of narrative voice will also be determined by your plot and by how you want to convey information to the reader.

1. What is going to be the dominant narrative voice for your story?
2. What does the reader need to know about
   a. the characters?
   b. the place?
   c. the events?
3. How are you going to reveal this information to the reader?
   a. Tell them directly
   b. Tell them through dialogue, letters, etc.
   c. Show them through description, imagery, etc.
4. Which piece of information is best conveyed in which way?

You know who your protagonist is, you know where your story is set and you know how you're going to convey information to the reader. Now's the time to start writing.

CHAPTER 5
THE NOIR

Author in the Spotlight: Lin Anderson
Chapter Focus: Plot points

A lot is happening in this extract from Lin Anderson's *Picture Her Dead*, and the information we are being given is serving a range of purposes. We are learning about the nitty-gritty of forensic procedures, about aspects of the main characters and about what has actually happened to the body that has been discovered. Lin Anderson has constructed the narrative very carefully to lead to that moment of discovery, the moment when the plot opens out and gains impetus. What does she do to make that moment stand out?

Roy set up the camera on its tripod, attached it to his laptop then eased a probe through the aperture. The first exposures began in darkness, gradually shifting to light.

They began to make out a narrow alcove. Against the lower half of this were the collapsed remains of a naked body. As the exposures lightened, they saw a mesh of silvery spider webs. The light from the lens provoked a flurry of activity amid the inhabitants and a long-legged spider took flight, escaping through the aperture to fall on to Rhona's hand. She shook it lightly to the floor, where it scuttled off at great speed, and focused back on the screen.

'Looks like the deceased was male,' said Chrissy. 'What's that across his chest?'

'Some kind of harness?' replied Rhona. The camera moved slowly upwards to glint off a semicircle of silver spikes. 'And a studded collar.'

'OK, I'm beginning to get the picture,' said Chrissy.

The scalp and hair had detached from the skull and slid forward to partially cover the eyes, as Rhona had seen when she'd first peered through the hole. Now she could make out the exposed cranium. It looked intact, with no obvious evidence of trauma. The human skull varies in thickness, with a thicker frontal area and the temporal region thinner and therefore more vulnerable to fracture.

'No obvious evidence of a fractured skull. Can you come down a little lower to the mouth?'

Rory did so.

'The tongue's still attached, and it's protrusive,' she noted. 'Can you focus on the neck?'

This was more difficult due to the collar. Rory moved the camera about.

'I can't see a ligature.'

'Unless the collar acted as one.'

'OK, let's take another look at the torso.'

The collapsing body had slumped at the waist, the legs folded sideways, the abdomen obscured by the bent legs. There were no obvious puncture holes from bullets or sharp implements in the brown-black leathery skin.

As they reached the lower half, the left hand came into view. It had broken free of the wrist, and now lay across the remains of the left knee.

'Hold it there.'

Rhona studied the image closely. The hand was shrivelled and dried out. Hanging loose on the forefinger was a chunky tarnished silver ring, but what interested her was the mangled state of the fingernails.

'Can you find the right hand?'

The camera scanned slowly across the torso.

'Stop there.'

The right hand was visible now, propped against the back wall.

'Give me a close-up on the fingernails, please.'

Roy zoomed in. Those that had not detached were also badly broken, several of them to half their normal length.

'So, what d'you think?' Chrissy said.

'No blunt-force wounds to the head. No obvious ligature. A protruding tongue and damaged nails and fingers.' Rhona paused. 'I'd hazard a guess and say he suffocated trying to claw his way out. Which might account for the loosened brick.'

'You mean the poor bastard was walled up alive?'

'It's a strong possibility.'

From *Picture Her Dead* by Lin Anderson

Why 'noir'? Literally 'black', it was a term that was used initially in the 1930s, both for the less socially optimistic and morally confident kind of hardboiled crime fiction, and for the despairing black-and-white movies made by refugees from Nazi Germany and Austria. There is no very clear origin to the term, though. However, its meaning in relation to crime fiction is now well established and widely understood to relate to those crime-fiction stories whose protagonists are in some way flawed, and whose overall vision tends, at the best, to the equivocal and, at the most extreme, to the deeply pessimistic.

There are a number of different sub-genres of noirs – American noirs, Mediterranean noirs, Tartan noirs . . . Lin Anderson is one of the prime exponents of the Tartan noir, although Ian Rankin, whom we discuss in Chapter 7 on police procedurals, is often cited as the king of the genre. Rankin, as it happens, chose Lin Anderson's first Rhona MacLeod book, *Driftnet*, as one of his top twenty favourite books.

Rhona MacLeod is a forensic scientist and a complex personality who has to deal with an awful lot. As Lin Anderson herself says of her protagonist, 'She's had a tough time so far, and it'll probably get worse before it gets better. Good job she's a strong, sexy woman . . .' MacLeod's professional life is based in Edinburgh and, as a forensic scientist, it is more often than not the darker, dingier and more dangerous parts of the city to which she is summoned. Anderson is adept at conjuring up the damp in the air, the grit underfoot, the grim, grey stone of the buildings and the grim, grey faces of their inhabitants. The world that MacLeod inhabits has no easy answers. The characters who people that world are confused, corrupt, frail and fallible, as well as committed to protecting the vulnerable, containing the wicked, and grasping at the possibilities of trust and happiness. As with hardboiled crime fiction, the reader knows that the central characters are on the side of the angels; but, unlike with hardboiled crime fiction, there is no guarantee that the angels will prevail . . .

The purpose of plot points and how to use them effectively

What I'd like concentrate on here, though, is less the darkness inherent to the noir genre than the construction of the plot and how to seed information to the reader – something Anderson does with great skill, as is clear from the passage quoted above.

In any story, there are a number of 'plot points' – moments when the trajectory of the narrative jumps or twists events into a new direction. One the major challenges for a writer is to make these moments plausible and convincing. Readers, quite reasonably, are not impressed by unlikely coincidences. Perhaps unfairly, real life provides many more far-fetched coincidences than any novelist could get away with. Equally, the plot point is most effective in terms of involving the reader if they can share the shock of discovery with the characters in the book.

In the passage above, for instance, a mummified body has been found behind a crumbling wall in a disused cinema. Rhona and her team have been called in to investigate. As the passage develops we are gradually taken from outside the alcove where the body has lain hidden right into the alcove and, finally, into a close-up of the dead man's fingers. The whole scene has an extraordinarily cinematic quality, which conveys graphically the details of the scene being described, the scientific detachment with which Rhona is viewing it, and the shock of the final revelation.

Making the reader do some of the work

How does Lin Anderson achieve this? First of all, by the objectivity with which we are invited to view the scene. There is no emotive language until Chrissy's exclamation at the end of the passage – the description is purely factual, the dialogue pragmatically instrumental. The only glance towards creepy (apart from the obvious unpleasantness of a mummified corpse) is the spider that runs across Rhona's hand, but this too is simply treated as a factual and unimportant occurrence – 'she shook it lightly to the floor' – rather than the stuff of horror movies. The effect of this very restrained writing is to make the reader have to do a lot of the work themselves, picturing in their own heads what the characters are seeing and bringing their own attempts at understanding to bear on the scene. We feel the shock almost as much as Chrissy when the implications finally become clear, 'You mean the poor bastard was walled up alive?', and the chill with Rhona's phlegmatic response, 'It's a strong possibility.'

The crucial thing about plot points is that they not only move the story forward but that they also have an emotional impact – what happens has to matter to the reader. To some extent, this is something that will grow naturally out of the way you write as you are going along, but it is worth having a clear idea from the beginning about where the turning points in your story are, how they will be revealed and how you will engage the reader in their discovery. In order to help you do this, you might find it useful to develop a range of different strategies that you can deploy, so that you can select the appropriate one from your toolkit when the time is right.

Using discoveries and revelations

Start by making a list of all the different ways in which things can be discovered – letters, emails, photographs, things (or bodies) being buried, hearsay . . . Make the list as long as you can – you may find unexpected ideas crop up, which will prove useful later on when you're getting down to the nitty-gritty of writing.

Next, make a second list of all the different ways in which these discoveries can be revealed to the reader – directly in the narrative, through what a character sees or finds, through what one character tells another . . . Again, make this list as exhaustive as you can – what you are doing is assembling a range of tools that you pick up and apply at the right time when you come to write.

Finally, have a look at your first list, decide on what your three or four pivotal moments of revelation are going to be, then choose from your second list how those moments are going to be discovered. Don't worry if you find these decisions being modified once you start writing – the idea is to develop a skeleton from which you can proceed with your story.

CORE EXERCISE: SEEDING INFORMATION

To play around with ways in which you might seed information for the reader, and then pick it up in such a way that hurls the plot forwards, perhaps in an unexpected direction, try writing two short paragraphs:

1. An opening paragraph in which you include information that doesn't look important at the time but is going to prove crucial later on in the story.

2. The paragraph in which that information is revealed as being important.

There are different ways in which discoveries and revelations can work in a story – they can be hinted at, implied or arrived at with a bang, giving the reader a shock. As writers, and particularly as crime-fiction writers, we have a tendency to be attracted to the flash-bang-wallop, rabbit-out-of-a-hat reveal. If we haven't sufficiently prepared the way, the drawback of the surprise being totally unexpected by the reader is that they will, quite reasonably, feel cross and betrayed. There is an unspoken contract between the reader and the writer that whatever happens within the world of the book will be consistent and plausible, in keeping with the kind of story being told and the kind of events being conjured up. To suddenly produce a *deus ex machina* – some unexpected, unprepared-for event – however ingenious, will smack of cheating to the reader, and the reader's trust, once lost, is hard, if not impossible to regain.

That is the first consideration. The second is related to pacing and plot construction. There are different ways of moving your plot forward and, depending on the kind of crime fiction you are writing, you will want to move at different speeds. Fundamentally, though, your plot is given a nudge by the introduction of a new event and/or new information.

Plot points are those moments that interrupt the movement of the story, give it a bit of a shake and set it off in a different direction. As always, though, you need to prepare the reader for the moment, even if it's only by preparing them to be surprised.

All of which is to say that, as a writer of noirs, and, indeed, of any kind of crime fiction, you need to mesh the fiendishly clever and unexpected twists and turns with what is possible within the world of the book, seeding ideas in your readers' minds so that the various revelations, when they come, are recognizable as well as a shock. Lin Anderson does this in the passage above by putting the shock into the voice of one of the characters, who speaks aloud, as it were, the reader's growing suspicions. Is this a technique you might use, do you think?

CHAPTER 6
THE THRILLER

Author in the Spotlight: Chris Carter
Chapter Focus: Pace and sentence structure

One of the most important elements in a thriller is the speed with which the story unfolds. This is partly achieved through the way in which the author develops the plot, but much more so through the way in which the story is told. This passage, which comes at the beginning of a chapter from fairly early on in Chris Carter's *The Executioner*, keeps the pressure on the reader from the opening sentence. How does he achieve that? You might find it interesting to read this passage aloud, and to observe the way in which your reading slows down and speeds up.

Amanda Reilly felt incredibly cold and thirsty. Her head thumped with such ferocity that she thought her temples would explode. As she tried to move she realised she was tied down. Her wrists had been bound to the arms and her ankles to the legs of an uncomfortable metal armchair – so tight the wires were cutting into her skin.

Her eyelids felt heavy and sticky. As far as she could tell she wasn't blindfolded, but something was keeping her from opening her eyes. She tried to scream but her lips wouldn't come apart. There was a bitter and sickening taste in her mouth. Instinctively, she pushed her tongue against her lips and felt a rigid, thin layer of something unidentified between them. She tried forcing her mouth open and felt the tender skin on her lips start to tear.

Oh my God!

Shivering, she finally understood what'd happened.

Her mouth had been super-glued shut.

From *The Executioner* by Chris Carter

Chris Carter writes his highly successful thrillers with the authority of first-hand knowledge. He was a forensic psychologist for a number of years before turning his hand to crime fiction. There are various things that set his writing apart – the unrelenting pace of his plots, the extreme savagery of his villains and the stark clarity of his sentences. Thrillers are at the extreme end of the crime-fiction continuum described in Chapter 1, characterized by the darkness of their vision, the violence of the action and the rapid pace of events. If we look briefly at this passage from Chris Carter's *The Executioner* we can begin to see how these effects are achieved.

Using simple sentences

The first thing to notice is Carter's sentence structure. Almost all the sentences he uses in this passage are **simple sentences**, and even where there are **compound sentences**, there are few qualifying **subordinate clauses**. Punctuation is kept to the barest minimum. The starkness of Carter's style is perhaps best brought out by comparing it with part of the passage from Ben Aaronovitch that is discussed in full in Chapter 11:

It started at one thirty on a cold Tuesday morning in January when Martin Turner, street performer and, in his own words, apprentice gigolo, tripped over a body in front of the West Portico of St Paul's at Covent Garden. Martin, who was none too sober himself, at first thought the body was that of one of the many celebrants who had chosen the Piazza as a convenient outdoor toilet and dormitory. Being a seasoned Londoner, Martin gave the body the 'London once-over' – a quick glance to determine whether this was a drunk, a crazy or a human being in distress. The fact that it was entirely possible for someone to be all three simultaneously is why good-Samaritanism in London is considered an extreme sport – like base-jumping or crocodile-wrestling. Martin, noting the good-quality coat and shoes, had just pegged the body as a drunk when he noticed that it was in fact missing its head.

Both writers are superb craftsmen, each aiming at very different effects. Aaronovitch's prose is leisured, measured, complex and witty, with all sorts of details piled one on another. Carter is concerned with focusing intently on the physical reality of the events being experienced by his character and witnessed by his readers. It would be an interesting exercise to write each passage in the style of the other, but almost impossible without adding substantial amounts of information that neither of the authors has given us. And this is because they are writing such very different kinds of books.

Choosing your weapons: different language, different effects

There is another thing that is highlighted by the differences between these two passages, as well as the contrast in their sentence structure, and that is the difference in the authors' choice of language. There is an extraordinary range of language and **lexicons** to choose from in English as a result of the patchwork pressures of our history. Fundamentally, we have at least three different palettes we draw on when writing: words with Anglo-Saxon roots, words with French/Norman/Latin roots, and words borrowed higgledy-piggledy from other languages.

Without going into too much detail, the differences between these various vocabularies have their roots in the comings and goings of peoples to these islands, and from these islands to other lands. Put simplistically, there are three main lexicons on which we can draw, and each has very different effects on the reader. Among the first peoples to inhabit the British Isles were the Celts – it is a sign of just how much they were oppressed, absorbed, pushed back and marginalized that the Celtic languages have left very little trace in our contemporary English. The Romans came and went relatively briskly, leaving their traces in place names but little else. Next, in terms of influential settlers, came the Angles and the Saxons, Germanic peoples who gave the English their name and a substantial proportion of their everyday language. The Roman influence on the other side of the Channel lasted much longer and went much deeper than it did in Britain, so that when the Normans jumped in their ships and defeated the Anglo-Saxons, they brought with them the Romance language of French. Not only that, but the language of the Church and of the law was Latin, and remained so for many centuries. Finally, we have the ragbag of borrowings from British imperial incursions to other lands, and from different groups of immigrants settling here – not to mention the increasing influence of the global culture of the new media.

What does this mean for the writer? Fundamentally it means that we have at our disposal a whole range of different lexicons, depending on the effects we want to achieve. Just to compare for a moment the different resonances of words drawn from Anglo-Saxon roots and words drawn from French/Norman/Latin roots. Words with Anglo-Saxon roots are direct, day-to-day words of naming and doing. Words with French/Norman/Latin roots provide the language of power – the language of the royal court and the law courts, the language of academics and experts. On the simplest of levels, if you want to create a scene or a character that is straightforward, clear and quickly understood, then it's usually best to use words with Anglo-Saxon roots. If you want to build atmosphere, or create a character who is obviously intellectual and clever, then drawing on our French/Norman/Latin inheritance will provide you with a range of useful tools.

If we look again at the passage from Chris Carter quoted above, it's interesting to pick out all the words he uses that draw on Anglo-Saxon roots: 'felt', 'cold', 'thirsty', 'head', 'thumped', 'thought'… And that's just in the first two sentences. Carter's use of predominantly Anglo-Saxon words, combined with his short, simple sentences, gives his writing speed, clarity and directness.

Setting the pace

Speed and directness are crucial to the thriller, not only in the author's use of language, of course, but also in the way in which the plot unfolds. What the reader is looking for is mounting tension, increasing horror, and shock following shock as the tempo quickens until the dramatic finale. It is important, though, to allow your reader time to relax as well. Think roller-coaster – you need the long slow grind of the ascent, bringing you closer and closer to the irreversible, heady descent, in order to recover from one headlong terrifying rush, and to savour the tremulous anticipation of the next. One technique that can prove helpful as you plan your book is to set out your scenes or chapters in a graph or bar chart, so that you can gauge the pace and tension of your plot, building to a dramatic crescendo, followed by the satisfaction of the final resolution, as the reader coasts towards the end of the ride.

CORE EXERCISE: TAKING THE TEMPERATURE OF THE BOOK

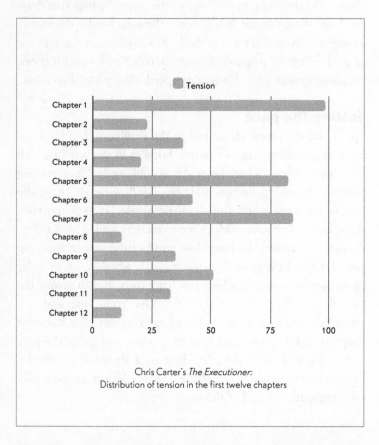

Chris Carter's *The Executioner:*
Distribution of tension in the first twelve chapters

Here, the x-axis represents the sequence of scenes in the book, while the y-axis indicates the intensity of the shock revealed in that scene. Here we are looking at how Chris Carter ratchets up the tension and horror in the opening few chapters of *The Executioner*. The book starts with a shock and a mystery, which Carter deftly interweaves with quieter and more humorous scenes that establish the characters involved in solving these serial killings and provide the reader with the necessary information to become increasingly engaged with the story.

So, what are the events you are going to be unfolding in your thriller? You might find it helpful to list them now, before you go any further, starting with a shock and then moving forward in an increasing crescendo of nastiness.

Once you've decided what the key events are, decide how you are going to place them throughout your book so that you build the tension towards a crescendo. Say you are going to be writing about 70,000 words, and you have ten key moments of terror/horror, you might want to distribute them something like this so that you are ratcheting up the tension and anticipation incrementally towards the finale:

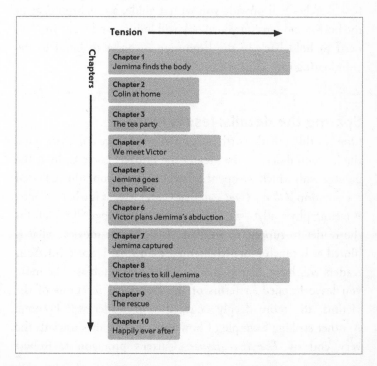

Tension ⟶

Chapters

Chapter 1
Jemima finds the body

Chapter 2
Colin at home

Chapter 3
The tea party

Chapter 4
We meet Victor

Chapter 5
Jemima goes
to the police

Chapter 6
Victor plans Jemima's abduction

Chapter 7
Jemima captured

Chapter 8
Victor tries to kill Jemima

Chapter 9
The rescue

Chapter 10
Happily ever after

You can see that this means your book starts with a bang, drops in tension, then gradually builds in an increasingly steep curve, with events following more and more rapidly one after another, until the climax, followed by a brief scene or two to wrap everything up and bring the reader back down to earth, satisfied that good has prevailed and evil has been banished, at least for the time being.

Finally, in preparation for writing the book as a whole, you might find it useful to write the first and last of your chosen key moments – the first, your opening scene, shocking, intriguing and slightly mysterious, catching the reader's attention and getting them hooked by not giving too much away; the last, resolving the situation in a final paroxysm of fear and horror. These won't be the scenes as they are finally published but these first sketches will provide you with a guide, a touchstone, as to the horror and tension your book will induce, and what you will need to hold back in the beginning in order to build to the culminating impact of the final key scene.

Sparing the details: less is more

One last thing that's worth bearing in mind – the more you state, the less you describe, the greater the impact. Look again at the passage with which we opened this chapter. Beyond the italicized exclamation '*Oh my God!*', all that Carter tells us is what Amanda is feeling physically – what that means psychologically is left for the reader to supply. In thrillers, as in horror movies, what is hinted at is much more frightening than what is spelt out. Your readers will have their own fears, their own phobias. The more you leave implied in terms of the emotional reactions of the victims, the more deeply engaged your reader will become. Another striking example of how this works comes towards the very end of *The Executioner*. Carter's protagonist, Robert

Hunter, is closing in on the Slasher. As he explores the darkened apartment where his antagonist is hiding, with at least one victim at his mercy, Hunter quite literally smells blood:

> He'd only taken a couple of steps when something made him stop dead. He picked up a heavy metallic scent and his heart sank. He knew that odor extremely well.
>
> *Blood.*
>
> From the strength of the smell he knew there was a lot of it. He spun around slowly, the beam of his flashlight searching everywhere. He almost choked when he finally saw her.
>
> 'Oh God, no.'
>
> She was naked and kneeling against the corner. Her breasts and abdomen covered in blood that'd cascaded from her slit throat.

There are only two brief indications of what Hunter is feeling – 'his heart sank', 'Oh God, no' – otherwise the horror of the scene is entirely conjured up through the physical description – what Hunter sees, what Hunter smells. The reader has to work hard to visualize the scene, and supplements Carter's description with their own imagination and emotional engagement. In the case of thriller writing, less really is more.

PART 2:
TAKING YOU
BEHIND THE SCENES

TECHNICAL FOCUS:
LANGUAGE AND DETAIL

CHAPTER 7
THE POLICE PROCEDURAL

Author in the Spotlight: Ian Rankin
Chapter Focus: Specialist vocabulary

One of the delights for the reader of police procedurals is the feeling that you are on the inside of a usually closed world, being made party to privileged information. Ian Rankin is a past master at this, and there are several layers of this kind of special insight being deployed in this passage from Rankin's *Saints of the Shadow Bible*. Rankin does this partly through the use of specialist vocabulary but also through the way in which he takes the reader behind the scenes or, in this case, behind police lines. What sense do you get of what it is like to be part of a major crime investigation in this passage?

Some of the same faces Clarke had seen outside the McCuskeys' home were now huddled on the narrow pavement on Torpichen Place. Cars and vans parked illegally were being ticketed by wardens, but without the owners seeming to mind. Those same vehicles had narrowed the road from three lanes to one, and traffic was backed up, giving drivers plenty of time to stare at the media circus.

Once inside the police station, having ignored all the questions yelled in her direction, Clarke showed her ID and was buzzed through a locked door into the body of the building. Every bit of space on the first floor seemed to be in the process of being taken over by the Major Incident Team – desks moved, extra chairs sought, communications established. Clarke squeezed her way through the melee until she reached its still centre and introduced herself to DCI Ralph. He was over six feet tall, his dark hair parted in the centre, and sporting a neatly trimmed beard. He didn't bother with a handshake or words of welcome, telling her instead that there would be a briefing in ten minutes' time and she should make herself useful until then.

'Olivia will show you the ropes,' he explained, nodding towards a young woman who was carrying a computer printer past him.

'Olivia Webster,' the officer said by way of introduction, as Clarke followed her. 'I'm a DC.'

'I'm DI Clarke.'

'Siobhan Clarke – I know who you are.'

'Have we met before?'

Webster shook her head. She had long brown hair and grey eyes, her skin pale. 'I've just heard you mentioned.' She placed the printer on one of the desks, next to a monitor. 'I've only been here six weeks – transferred from Dundee.' She stared at the set-up on the desk.

'Keyboard?' Clarke suggested.

Webster smiled. 'Knew something wasn't quite right.' She scanned the room. 'Must be one around here somewhere . . .' Then she was off again, leaving Clarke without any sense of what she should or shouldn't be doing. She peered from a window until the press pack below noticed her and started waving.

'Not much room here for media conferences.' DCI Ralph was standing next to her. 'We're using the hotel on the corner instead.'

'Good thinking.'

He studied her. 'You were at the scene soon after Mr McCuskey was found.' Statement rather than question. 'That's why I want you to focus on the break-in itself – the nuts and bolts, if you like.'

Clarke nodded her acceptance. 'There's already an officer working on the stolen goods – putting word out.'

'Good.'

'Maybe we could bring him in?'

'As part of the team, you mean?' He wafted a hand in the general direction of the chaos behind him. 'You think we're short-staffed?'

'Just seems rational, since he's been involved in the preliminary investigation.'

'This wouldn't be your old friend, would it? The infamous John Rebus?'

'John not only has contacts, he was also with me when we attended the scene of a crash not far from the McCuskey home. The young woman pulled from the wreckage happens to be Forbes McCuskey's girlfriend. We're not sure she was alone in the car at the time.'

Ralph grew thoughtful. 'That's quite the coincidence.'

'Our thinking exactly. Again, if DS Rebus is brought in, he's already done a lot of the groundwork . . .'

'Let me think about it, once I've got the pep talk out of the way.'

From *Saints of the Shadow Bible* by Ian Rankin

All the four genres we are looking at in the 'Taking You Behind the Scenes' section of this book depend for their appeal on providing insights into worlds and ways of seeing and behaving to which we, the readers, do not normally have access. We are shown events and actions, character and behaviour from a new and unfamiliar perspective, in a way that both takes us behind the scenes into areas of specialist expertise and also reveals the pressures and problems to which the experts in those areas are subject.

In the passage quoted above, there is, as always with Ian Rankin, a great deal going on and a lot of information being given to the reader in an apparently effortless and seemingly entirely natural way. As well as being a past master of the noir genre (or Tartan noir, as Rankin himself has dubbed it), Ian

Rankin is also highly skilled at developing police procedurals in which the ways that the police choose or are constrained to behave are an integral part of the story. It is worth looking at this passage in some detail in order to see just what it is that Rankin is telling the reader, how that information is being conveyed and what we, as writers, can learn from Rankin's great skill in this regard.

The first thing to notice is that Rankin is presenting the scene in third-person narrative but from the point of view of Siobhan Clarke. We see things through her eyes, as she sees them – we know what she knows, we feel what she feels.

The second thing to focus on is that a substantial proportion of the information is provided through the dialogue.

Mimicking life

These two techniques together create a sense of naturalness and of familiarity. In ordinary life, we ourselves gather information through what we observe ourselves and through conversation with others. Rankin's narrative technique convincingly mimics our own lived experience. He does, however, manage to tell us a great deal and to move the story on, without directly addressing us, narrator to reader, at all. So what is it that we learn and how?

We know, through Siobhan's own observations, that we are now at the police station, which, since the murder of McCuskey, a government minister seen slightly earlier in the book, is now surrounded by an excited pack of newshounds. The chaos outside the police station is deftly conjured up by the vehicles parked any old where across the road, their drivers indifferent to the parking fines since it's not they who will be paying them. Much more important to the journalists is getting a story. Then, once we follow Siobhan into the police station, we are made aware of the intense activity as the incident room is set up, not because of what anyone says but because of what Siobhan sees. Siobhan is an experienced police officer so she knows what to expect and so we, as readers, learn what to expect by, as it were, walking beside her. We see the preoccupation of the officer in charge. We learn about the ad hoc nature of putting together resources for this kind of operation under pressure of time – DC Webster, a virtual stranger to the building, rooting around for the equipment that will be needed. We find out, through DCI Ralph informing Siobhan, that there will be a press conference in a separate location. Finally, and perhaps most importantly in terms of the way in which the plot moves forward, we see the delicacy of the relationships between the different members of the operation, and how Siobhan seeks to draw John Rebus into the team, but cannot do so except tangentially, since it is up to DCI Ralph to make the decisions. The subtlety of the relationship between Siobhan and Rebus is deftly captured in the short exchange between Ralph and Siobhan, in which she gives her superior an interesting piece of information, and she follows up by emphasizing Rebus's role as part of the team that discovered it in the delicately phrased, 'Our thinking exactly.'

So what is there in Rankin's handling of the police procedural here that we as writers can learn from?

CORE EXERCISE: DECIDING WHAT MATTERS

Fundamentally, it is a question of deciding what matters in terms of the story and including only those elements that are essential to making the story work. There is a great temptation for us as writers to over-describe and over-explain – and there are, of course, occasions when both description and explanation are essential. Much less often than you would think, though, particularly when, as with Rankin here, you are allowing the reader to look over the shoulders of the characters as they go about their business in a world that to them is entirely familiar.

One way of testing out whether this technique could work for you is to write a passage fairly fully, and then pare it down to the bare essentials. I would suggest writing about yourself coming home in the evening, covering perhaps the first half-hour to an hour of your return to your house or flat. Write about yourself in the third person to create a slight sense of distance. Do this exercise in several stages:

1. Write your account as fully and in as much detail as possible.
2. Rewrite it, taking out any details that do not add to your reader's understanding of what you're describing.
3. Create a second character, and have them greet you when you get home.
4. Create a dialogue between the two of you.

Now look through all four versions of your account – what is different? What have you chosen to dispense with? What does your reader absolutely have to know in order to understand what is happening? There will be elements of your home, and your homecoming, that are distinctive to you. There are other elements that can be taken for granted or at least only alluded to lightly. How do you select which is which, and how does their inclusion or removal affect the way in which your account reads?

To turn back briefly to the passage from Ian Rankin with which we opened this chapter, we can see that Rankin includes nothing that Siobhan, through whose eyes we are seeing the scene, would herself take for granted as ordinary and familiar.

Using selective description

We receive no description of the police station – Siobhan knows it well already. We do receive a description of DCI Ralph, as this is the first time Siobhan has met him. What this means for your police procedural is that you need to maintain an awareness of what your characters know and take for granted. Don't describe in detail elements with which your characters would already be entirely familiar. The more you include your reader as a companion or colleague of your characters, rather than an outsider who needs to be fed information, the more they will become engaged with and involved in your story. It's little spoken about, but readers actually don't mind doing quite a lot of work so long as the rewards are there for them as well . . . Reward them with an intriguing and exciting story, and they'll happily settle down with your characters, their knowledge and the way they see the world.

CHAPTER 8
THE FORENSIC

Author in the Spotlight: Patricia Cornwell
Chapter Focus: Technical detail

The passage below is taken from fairly early on in Patricia Cornwell's *Red Mist*. In it, Cornwell is doing a number of things – introducing her protagonist, Kay Scarpetta, to those who may not have encountered her before, but also, as importantly, quite clearly setting out the nature of her specialist knowledge and the importance of its precision. It is interesting, as you read through, to pick out just how many specialist terms Cornwell uses in this short passage.

> Most people refer to me as a medical examiner, an ME, but some think I'm a coroner, and occasionally I'm confused with a police surgeon. To be precise, I'm a physician with a specialty in pathology, and subspecialties in forensic pathology and 3-D imaging radiology, or the use of CT scans to view a dead body internally before I touch it with a blade. I have a law degree and the special reservist rank of colonel with the Air Force, and therefore an affiliation with the Department of Defense, which last year appointed me to head the Cambridge Forensic Center it has funded in conjunction with the Commonwealth of Massachusetts, the Massachusetts Institute of Technology (MIT), and Harvard.
>
> I'm an expert at determining the mechanism of what kills or why something doesn't, whether it is a disease, a poison, a medical misadventure, an act of God, a handgun, or an improvised explosive device (IED). My every action has to be

legally well informed. I'm expected to assist the United States government as needed and directed. I swear to oaths and testify under them, and what all this means is that I'm really not entitled to live the way most people do. It isn't an option for me to be anything other than objective and clinical. I'm not supposed to have personal opinions or emotional reactions in any case, no matter how gruesome or cruel. Even if violence has impacted me directly, such as the attempt on my life four months ago, I'm to be as unmoved as an iron post or a rock. I'm to remain hard in my resolve, calm and cool.

'You're not going to go PTSD on me, are you?' the chief of the Armed Forces Medical Examiners, General John Briggs, said to me after I was almost murdered in my own garage this past February 10. 'Shit happens, Kay. The world is full of whack jobs.'

'Yes, John. Shit happens. Shit has happened before, and shit will happen again,' I replied, as if all were fine and I'd taken everything in stride, when I knew that wasn't what I was feeling inside.

From *Red Mist* by Patricia Cornwell

In the world of fiction writing, there is one combination of techniques that is utterly fundamental to engaging the reader and moving the story along. It is used by all fiction writers of whatever genres in different proportions, depending on their style and purpose. This is the combination of the techniques of **showing** and **telling**. There is no right or wrong about the proportions of showing and telling you use as a writer – it depends very much on your reader's expectations and on what you are trying to achieve. In forensic crime fiction, as in legal and courtroom crime fiction, there is to some extent a need to veer towards the 'telling' end of things, since the majority of your readers will be non-specialists, intrigued by the details of worlds that they know about, but to which they have no access. The difficulty that arises with simply telling your reader things is that they are likely to get bored very quickly – so you need to make sure that all the information you are giving is actually both crucial to the story and also serves to draw your reader in – engage as well as inform.

There are a number of ways of doing this, and we'll be looking at two or three techniques that you may find useful, but, before we start, it's worth having a close look at how Patricia Cornwell, the well-established queen of forensic crime fiction, goes about bringing her readers up to speed in the opening chapter of *Red Mist*.

Addressing the reader

The first thing to remark is that Kay Scarpetta, the first-person narrator, appears to be speaking directly to the reader. This is an unusual technique for a first-person narrative, as it risks breaking through the conventions of storytelling, which tend to assume a world of the book separate from the world of the reader. Occasionally, of course, authors breach the divide between the two, as in Charlotte Brontë's famous, 'Reader, I married him.' Usually, though, first-person narrators provide information to their readers in the form of diaries, letters, notes or dialogue between characters, rather than through directly addressing the reader. The advantage, of course, is that you have an easy and straightforward way of providing the reader with the information that they will need in order for you to be able to move the story forward. The disadvantage, and it is a substantial one, is that too much information delivered cold, as it were, can prove very indigestible and readers are likely to turn away.

Before we look in detail at the range of techniques for telling available to you, it is worth glancing a little more closely at just how much information Patricia Cornwell manages to impart to the reader in those four short paragraphs.

The first paragraph deals entirely with Kay Scarpetta's professional status in such a way that we are given all her qualifications and her military rank. What makes this palatable to the reader is the way in which Cornwell opens the paragraph: 'Most people refer to me as a medical examiner . . .' This immediately puts the reader in the position of being on the inside, having the right information and using the right terms, rather than those who 'confuse' her role with that of a coroner or a police surgeon. The second paragraph appears at first to be in the same vein – providing the reader with specific information about what a medical examiner actually does, but then Cornwell gradually moves the focus from the general – this is what any ME does – to the particular – this is what I, Kay Scarpetta, recently experienced, and both how I am supposed to feel about it and also how I actually feel about it.

The next two paragraphs, which are mainly dialogue, again provide us with a range of information. Kay is on first-name terms with the general in charge of the Armed Forces Medical Examiners. He, it is implied, is not particularly sympathetic to emotional responses to trauma – 'You're not going to go PTSD on me, are you?' Finally, the narrator shows us a rift between Kay's pragmatic outward self-presentation – 'Yes, John. Shit happens.' – and her inner turmoil. The reader is left with the feeling, by the end of this short passage, that Kay Scarpetta's inner feelings, and her hidden vulnerability, are going to play a large part in the story to come.

Making statements

Almost all of this information is given to the reader directly, through statements, and this is certainly a possible route to take when writing this kind of crime fiction. I would suggest, however, that it is a fairly high-level skill to handle this kind of direct relationship with the reader successfully. For the majority of us, it is probably safer to embed the providing of information within the world of the story, using one of the writer's trusty friends, the 'uninformed outsider' or the 'innocent eye' (which can, of course, be one and the same character).

Before looking at which character might play this role in your story, and how to make use of them so that they're not just standing there as a stooge for your clever forensic specialist, it's crucial to get an idea of what kind of forensic specialism you are going to be unfolding, so that you can decide just what information your reader is going to need to have at their disposal (and how much research you yourself are going to have to do). The substantial majority of current forensic crime-fiction novels have as their protagonists MEs or forensic pathologists, but what about all the other forensic disciplines available to you? Here's a brief list of just some of the specialisms your protagonist could be expert in:

- Forensic pathology
- Forensic entomology
- Forensic botany
- Forensic psychology
- Forensic psychiatry
- Forensic anthropology
- Forensic radiology
- Forensic dentistry
- Forensic paediatrics
- Computer forensics

And, of course, there are more . . .

Providing specialist focus

Once you have settled on the specialism that will provide the solution to whatever criminal puzzle you are going to conjure up, it is worth spending a little time mapping out how your protagonist came to be involved in that field, what makes it distinctive from other areas of forensics and just what are the crucial clues that your expert will discover. You might find it helpful to make a few notes now to give you some starting points for when you write:

1. Background
2. Relevant specialist knowledge
3. Crucial clues they discover

There are a couple of other areas that you will probably find it helpful to have considered before you settle down to write.

Selecting the information

First of all, now that you know which forensic specialism is going to be at the heart of your book, and now that you also know what particular information this specialism will provide in order to solve the crime, it will be helpful for you to spend a little time charting just what kind of information the reader will need to have in order to follow the story, and then, on the basis of that, what you yourself will need to research. I like to regard this part of preparing to write as if it were a bit like building an iceberg – you need to know far more than you ever reveal to your reader; there needs to be substantially more below the waterline, so to speak, so that the story stays afloat.

1. Key events
2. Key evidence
3. Key forensic information
4. What the reader needs to know/understand
5. What needs to be researched
6. Who/what to turn to for that information

Finally, you will need to think about how you are going to provide this information to the reader without forcing them to follow a quick course in whatever forensic specialism you have selected for your protagonist. This is where the joys of the omniscient narrator can really come into play extremely helpfully. Being able to skip from perspective to perspective of your different characters means that you can reveal the confusion of one character, who stands in for the reader, and then have your protagonist clarify what is happening, what they have found and why it matters, in question and answer dialogue that makes the information accessible and relevant to the reader. This also ensures that what we are being told helps move the story forward.

CORE EXERCISE: SHOWING AND TELLING 1 – TELLING

So think now about who your 'innocent eye' might be, what role they play in the plot and what kind of questions it would be appropriate and helpful for them to ask. Select a key scene where the forensic findings are crucial to the solving of the mystery, and then note down very briefly what the findings are, why they matter and what questions a layperson would ask.

1. Outline a key scene
2. List forensic findings and what they show
3. List the questions a layperson would ask

As a last exercise before you set out on your own writing, look again at the passage from Patricia Cornwell with which we opened this chapter, and rewrite it as a dialogue between Kay Scarpetta and, say, a journalist interviewing her for a feature article. What is gained and what is lost by providing the information in dialogue form, rather than directly to the reader as Cornwell does? What are the different benefits of the different ways of telling?

CHAPTER 9
LEGAL FICTION

Author in the Spotlight: Michael Connelly
Chapter Focus: Insider view

One of Michael Connelly's great strengths as a writer of legal crime fiction is in bringing the highly technical and rather daunting world of the courtroom to life in such a way that the reader is not only introduced to the issues but also led to understand why they matter. It's interesting to see, in the passage below, how Connelly reveals not only the actualities of court procedure but also the human implications of that procedure.

The jury came out in a single-file like the Lakers taking the basketball court. They weren't all wearing the same uniform but the same feeling of anticipation was in the air. The game was about to begin. They split into two lines and moved down the two rows of the jury box. They carried steno pads and pens. They took the same seats they were in on Friday when the jury was completed and sworn in.

It was almost ten a.m. Monday and a later-than-expected start. But earlier, Judge Stanton had had the lawyers and the defendant back in chambers for almost forty minutes while he went over last-minute ground rules. [...]

Stanton was very interested in budgeting time for the trial. Like any judge, he had to keep things moving. He had a backlog of cases, and a long trial only backed things up further. He wanted to know how much time each side expected to take putting forth his case. Golantz said he would take a minimum of a week and I said

I needed much the same, though realistically I knew I would probably take much less time. Most of the defence case would be made, or at least set up, during the prosecution phase.

Stanton frowned at the time estimates and suggested that both the prosecution and defence think hard about streamlining. He said he wanted to get the case to the jury while their attention was still high.

From The Brass Verdict by Michael Connelly

In crime-fiction novels that are 'taking you behind the scenes', as courtroom and legal crime fiction does, there is a choice as to how you position the reader – are they an outsider, looking in and marvelling at the skill and knowledge of the protagonist (this is, by and large, the stance usually taken in forensic crime fiction), or are they seeing the events through the eyes of the protagonist, taking on their knowledge at the same time as adopting their point of view? This is very much the stance taken by Michael Connelly here, in a passage from a recent volume in his Mickey Haller, the Lincoln Lawyer, series. We are being given a lot of specialist information, but conversationally, almost anecdotally, as if from one friend to another. This has the effect of placing the reader on the inside, almost shoulder to shoulder with the expert protagonist, so that a lot of what is happening and what it means in terms of the events of the book is alluded to and implied, rather than explained.

What the reader learns

Let's take a brief moment to look at three things from this short extract from The Brass Verdict: what we learn, how we learn it and what it means in terms of the unfolding plot and the reader's understanding of what is happening.

1. What we learn:
    *   It's the first day of a jury trial.
    *   The judge has met counsel and the defendant in chambers in order to find out how long the prosecution and defence will need to present their cases.
    *   The judge is under pressure to get the trial out of the way as quickly as possible.
    *   The success of a jury trial depends on a number of factors.
2. How we learn it:
    *   'The game was about to begin.'
    *   'They took the same seats they were in on Friday when the jury was completed and sworn in.'
    *   'Judge Stanton had had the lawyers and the defendant back in chambers for almost forty minutes.'
    *   'He had a backlog of cases, and a long trial only backed things up further.'
    *   'He wanted to get the case to the jury while their attention was still high.'
3. What it means:
    *   In this first paragraph, Connelly manages to get a surprising amount of information to the reader while apparently saying very little. The important fact – it's the first day of the trial – is never actually stated. What we are told explicitly is that the jury came into court single file looking, to the narrator's eye, like a basketball team. This is further emphasized by the sentence, 'The game was about to begin.' It's a murder trial, but it's also, at an important level, a game. A game for the jurors, who have been taken out of their ordinary lives to participate in something unfamiliar and exciting; a game, too, for lawyers like Mickey Haller, who will bend the rules in order to win – though Connelly is very careful to have Haller only get the good guys off. The sense of theatre, of

play, of competition, rules and rule-breaking, is all implied in this opening paragraph through the use of simile and **metaphor.** There is also a very deft point made about the jury, which I will come back to in a minute.

- It is clear that the judge, Judge Stanton, is a crucial figure in the trial, and in how Mickey Haller will approach it. Stanton's absolute power within the courtroom is conveyed to the reader by the way in which he has held back the start of the trial by forty minutes in order to establish 'last-minute ground rules'.

- Having given the reader a sense of the authority of the judge, Connelly then shows just how much pressure Stanton is under as well, with a backlog of cases, which means that he needs to balance justice with practicality – another hint that, in the narrator's view, the law is something of a game, a compromise between what is wanted and what can be achieved.

- Finally, we have Mickey Haller's and Judge Stanton's views of the jury. There is a sense of fondness but also of condescension in the narrator's description of the jury filing into the jury box, eager with anticipation, their brand-new pens and writing pads held at the ready. Stanton's view seems rather more cynical, or perhaps pragmatic would be fairer. He doesn't believe a jury can concentrate properly through a long trial so he wants them to have to come to a verdict while everything is still fresh in their minds.

All of this information and all of these attitudes are shared with the reader as though they too are insiders. It's all taken for granted and doesn't need explaining. This gives the reader a privileged position in terms of an assumed understanding of the law, of courtrooms and of the ways in which they work. Rather than being dazzled by the protagonist's expertise, as in Patricia Cornwell's books and many other forensic crime novels, we are invited inside the tent to sit comfortably side by side with the protagonist, sharing their views.

CORE EXERCISE: POSITIONING THE READER

This is a very interesting and powerful narrative technique, and it may be one with which you'd like to experiment. To this end, I have included here a short law report of a case held before the Administrative Court in 2010. (For those who wish to follow the story of these legal proceedings further, there was an appeal held before Lord Justice Maurice Kay in the Court of Appeal (Civil Division) in 2012.) The report recounts the case of a young man in a young offender institution who had failed to comply with a prison officer's instructions and had therefore been disciplined by the governor by being held in solitary confinement in his cell for three days. The question before Lord Justice Pitchford and Justice Maddison was whether this constituted a breach of the young man's human rights, insofar as the right of association can be seen as a civil right.

What I'd like to suggest is that you read through this report, paying particular attention to the language in which it is written and the findings that it recounts, and then experiment by writing your own version of these events, following as far as possible Connelly's narrative technique, by positioning your reader as a trusted colleague who will have an interest and an understanding of the issues involved.

Regina (King) v Secretary of State for Justice [2010] EWHC 2522 (Admin); [2010] WLR (D) 258 (Prepared by the law reporters of the Incorporated Council of Law Reporting – www.iclr.co.uk)

DC: Pitchford LJ, Maddison J: 13 October 2010

The discretion of a prison governor to decide the extent of an inmate's basic association with his fellows did not remove from association its quality as a personal right, a right which was subject to the lawful exercise of discretion by the governor. Within the autonomous meaning afforded to civil rights by the European Court of Human Rights, a prisoner's residual right of association was a 'civil right' within art 6(1) of the Convention for the Protection of Human Rights and Fundamental Freedoms

The Divisional Court of the Queen's Bench Division so held in dismissing a claim by the claimant, Ben King, for judicial review of the decisions of Matthew Shepherd, the governor adjudicator and deputy head of residence at HM Prison Portland, dated 11 April 2009, that the claimant was guilty of a disciplinary offence while serving a sentence of detention at the Young Offender Institute at HM Prison Portland and should be confined in his cell for three days.

PITCHFORD LJ said that the argument placed before the court, that a prisoner's residual right to association, if established, was a civil right requiring the procedural guarantees of the civil limb of art 6(1) of the Convention for the Protection of Human Rights and Fundamental Freedoms, had not been addressed in R (Greenfield) v Secretary of State for the Home Department [2001] 1 WLR 1731 or R (Al-Hasan) v Secretary of State for the Home Department [2002] 1 WLR 545. His Lordship applied R v Board of Visitors of Hull Prison, Ex p St Germain [1979] QB 425, which had been concerned with the jurisdiction of the courts to intervene in the disciplinary process in Hull Prison but served to emphasise that the prisoner was not without rights to the extent that they were compatible with the sentence lawfully imposed. When a person received a custodial sentence, although he forfeited the freedom to associate with whomever he wished, he did not forfeit his right of association with all his fellow human beings and receive a sentence of solitary confinement. The discretion of the governor to decide the extent of the inmate's basic association with his fellows did not remove from association its quality as a personal right, which was a right which was subject to the lawful exercise of discretion by the governor. A prisoner had a right of access to a court if he asserted that the governor had arbitrarily removed from him any association with those of his fellow inmates with whom he would normally enjoy joint activities. The right of access to the courts existed because association was one of those residual rights which the prisoner retained subject to the lawful exercise of disciplinary powers or other powers. That was the distinction between the case of a prisoner and the case of the disciplinary recipient of a welfare or other benefit. When what was asserted as a right was no more than an argument that discretion or evaluative judgment should be exercised in the citizen's favour, it could not be classified as a civil right. The citizen's right was only to have the claim to the benefit considered fairly. This claimant was not in such a position and said he had the same basic right of association with his fellow inmates as they enjoyed subject to the lawful exercise of disciplinary power by the governor. Within the autonomous meaning afforded to civil rights by the European Court of Human Rights, a right of association in the sense described was a civil right. In his Lordship's judgment, on the facts of the present case, the proceedings complied with the requirements of fairness under art 6(1). The High Court enjoyed 'full' jurisdiction to review the issues which arose for consideration.

MADDISON J gave a concurring judgment.

Appearances: Philippa Kaufmann (instructed by Irwin Mitchell LLP) for the claimant; Sam Grodzinski (instructed by Treasury Solicitor) for the defendant.

Reported by: Georgina Orde, barrister

How did you find doing that exercise? What does that kind of narrative technique give you, as a writer? It seems to me that it's a very powerful way of creating a bond between the narrator and the reader, so that they will be strongly committed to wanting the protagonist to succeed, partly because we, as readers, feel ourselves to be in a privileged position inside the abstruse and usually hidden world of the law, rather than on the outside looking in. It is also a technique that demands a lot from the writer in terms of their knowledge and understanding of the specialist world into which they are inviting their readers. The iceberg principle alluded to in Chapter 8 is even more powerfully in play here – in order to provide your reader with the sense of a secure bed of shared knowledge, you do actually have to know your stuff pretty thoroughly.

CHAPTER 10
THE SPY NOVEL

Author in the Spotlight: Charles Cumming
Chapter Focus: Implication and explanation

It is not by chance that Charles Cumming's writing style so closely matches the substance of what he is writing about. The world of espionage is a world of shadows, of hints, of lies and innuendo. It is appropriate, then, that Cumming reveals a lot about his characters and plots by implication, rather than by spelling things out. When reading through the passage below, keep an eye out for how much we learn without actually being told.

Christopher Keen had taken the call personally in his private office. It was a routine enquiry, of the sort he handled every day, from a businessman calling himself Bob Randall with 'a minor difficulty in the former Soviet Union'.

'I've been informed,' Randall explained, 'that Russia is your area of expertise.'

Keen did not ask who had recommended him for the job. That was simply the way the business worked: by reputation, by word of mouth. Neither did he enquire about the nature of the problem. That was simply common sense when speaking on an open line. Instead, he said, 'Yes. I worked in the Eastern Bloc for many years.'

'Good.' Randall's voice was nasal and bureaucratically flat. He suggested a meeting in forty-eight hours at a location on the Shepherd's Bush Road.

'It's a Café Rouge, in the French style. On the corner of Batoum Gardens.' Randall spelt out 'Batoum' very slowly, saying 'B for Bertie' and 'A for Apple' in a way that tested Keen's patience. 'There are tables there which can't be seen from the street. We're not likely to be spotted. Would that be suitable for you, or do you have a specific procedure that you would like to follow?'

Keen made a note of the date in his desk diary and smiled: first-time buyers were often like this, jumpy and prone to melodrama, wanting codewords and gadgets and chalk marks on walls.

'There is no specific procedure,' he said. 'I can find the café.'

'Good. But how will I recognise you?'

As he asked the question, Bob Randall was sitting in Thames House staring at a JPEG of Keen taken in Western Afghanistan in 1983, but it was necessary cover.

'I'm tall,' Keen said, switching the phone to his other ear. 'I'll be wearing a dark suit, most probably. My experience is that in circumstances such as these two people who have never met before very quickly come to recognise one another. Call it one of the riddles of the trade.'

'Of course,' Randall replied. 'Of course. And when shall we say? Perhaps six o'clock?'

'Fine,' Keen said. He was already hanging up. 'Six o'clock.'

From *The Hidden Man* by Charles Cumming

Spy crime fiction appropriately occupies a kind of twilight zone. To some extent, all spy fiction is crime fiction, since espionage involves subterfuge and transgression, suborning and treachery, but not all spy fiction has criminal activity at the core of the plot. Assuming, then, that your spy novel will have one or more crimes, the solving of which is central to your story, what is it about writing spy crime fiction that makes it so distinctive?

If we look a little at the passage from Charles Cumming above, we can begin to get some idea of how this kind of crime-fiction writing can work when it's done well and how we might apply similar techniques to our own writing.

Using smoke and mirrors

Charles Cumming is a superb writer of British spy fiction, in the tradition of such formidable forerunners as Eric Ambler and John le Carré. Like le Carré, Cumming evokes a murky, ambiguous world, in which the characters routinely deceive each other and withhold information – and in which the reader has to negotiate layers of information and disinformation to reach any kind of idea about what is going on.

This passage from *The Hidden Man* opens with us being presented with events from the point of view of Christopher Keen. We immediately get a sense that Keen is involved in something not entirely above board, something, perhaps, to do with espionage. There is the mention of 'the former Soviet Union', the reference to the way 'the business worked: by reputation . . .', and there is the matter-of-fact acceptance that you didn't delve too deeply into things 'on an open line'.

We get an idea of what Keen is like – impatient, perhaps slightly patronizing – 'first-time buyers were often like this'. We get the sense that he is in control.

That all changes in the next paragraph, when the reader suddenly learns that it is Bob Randall who is not all that he seems. To Keen, he has presented himself in a voice that was 'nasal and bureaucratically flat', and has asked the questions that Keen expects of a 'first-time buyer'. In fact, though, Bob Randall is sitting in Thames House, the London headquarters of MI5, with a photo of Christopher Keen on the screen in front of him. Not only that, but we learn that Keen had been in Afghanistan at the time of the Soviet Afghan War – on whose side, and doing what, we have, at this point, no idea.

Cumming skilfully takes the reader in one direction, showing things from Keen's point of view, and then turns the whole situation around, presenting events from the point of view of the MI5 officer, stringing Keen along from his office in Thames House.

At no point, though, is the reader told what is happening – we have to work it out from the fragmentary information we are being drip-fed by the author. If Patricia Cornwell, in Chapter 8, appeared to be the queen of telling, Cumming proves himself here extraordinarily adept at the tricky art of showing.

Showing, rather than telling, working by implication rather than explanation, is a narrative technique particularly suited to the world of spy crime fiction, where very little is as it seems on the surface. But what does that mean for us as writers?

The techniques of showing

Cumming uses a range of techniques from which we can usefully learn – and which we can adapt for use in our own writing.

1. The first of these is a very specific use of the omniscient narrator. By definition, the omniscient narrator knows everything that is going on in the characters' minds. Here, though, we are shown *only* what is going on in the characters' minds – there is no 'helicopter view' from which to assess them, their feelings and actions. This means that the reader knows only what the characters know.
2. Secondly, Cumming moves from the point of view of one character to the point of view of another – we begin to piece the picture together through the contrast between the characters' viewpoints and the extra information we can gradually slot into place.
3. Finally, Cumming uses specific 'insider' information, without explaining it, which gives the reader a further task

of making sense of these terms and putting them into position in our understanding of what is actually happening in the narrative. 'Open line', 'codewords', 'Thames House', 'cover' – all these terms belong to the world of British espionage but nowhere are they explained. Why should they be? The characters know what they mean.

Before going on to develop ways of using similar techniques of showing in your own work, it's worth spending a little time thinking about your crime-fiction story: when and where it's set, what it's going to be about, who your characters are, what they know, what they don't know and, perhaps most important of all, what they'd really, really like to know.

The world of espionage, after all, is the world of knowledge – knowledge hidden, knowledge withheld, knowledge discovered, used, manipulated . . . So what is known, what is hidden and what is sought after are all crucial elements of any spy story.

So, what is the secret that matters, that lies at the heart of everything?

1. The secret
2. Why is it important?
3. Who knows it?
4. Who wants it?

Having sorted out the crucial piece of information that everyone is scrabbling over, make some more notes about who your main characters are and what role they play in relation to that information.

- Do they know it?
- Do they want it?
- Do they know it but don't know how valuable it is?
- Who has access to it?
- How is it going to be guarded?
- How is it going to be discovered?

Finally, now that you've got the main components of your plot – the people, the core information, how it's defended, how it's discovered – choose a scene to work on in which you have at least two characters involved, each of which know completely different parts of the puzzle.

CORE EXERCISE: SHOWING AND TELLING 2 – SHOWING

This exercise works best carried out in three stages:

1. Simply narrate your scene as an omniscient narrator, creating your two characters, what they're thinking, what they say and what they do.
2. Take your initial account of this scene and remove everything that the reader is told by the omniscient narrator. You will probably be left with a rather bare and disjointed set of comments, with the occasional piece of dialogue, but this is actually the point at which things get really interesting.
3. Look at the information that you have taken out, and explore how you can provide the reader with that information solely through the characters' thoughts, emotions, speech and actions.

By having two or more characters who actually don't know what the other characters are thinking, and by not providing the reader with that information through the voice of an omniscient narrator, you are doing two very powerful things:

1. You are making the reader work much harder so they get much more closely involved in the scene and characters you are describing.
2. You are making the reader have to work out what is going on in much the same way that the characters in your story are

having to fight their way through to some kind of clarity. In this way, your reader is drawn to sympathize on a very deep level with the characters, and particularly with your protagonist, since they are going on this journey of discovery side by side.

This probably isn't a technique you should use unremittingly throughout your story but, when you do use it, it can prove very powerful, and is particularly fitting for the murky and confused world of the spy crime-fiction novel.

PART 3:
TAKING YOU AWAY FROM THE WORLD YOU KNOW

TECHNICAL FOCUS:
PLACE AND DIALOGUE

CHAPTER 11
THE PARANORMAL

Author in the Spotlight: Ben Aaronovitch
Chapter Focus: Evoking place

The passage below comes from the very opening pages of Ben Aaronovitch's *The Rivers of London*. As you read through, keep a mental note of all the things that seem to you to build up a very ordinary scene, and of those few things that suggest something entirely out of the ordinary. What effect do these contrasting elements have on you as you're reading?

> It started at one thirty on a cold Tuesday morning in January when Martin Turner, street performer and, in his own words, apprentice gigolo, tripped over a body in front of the West Portico of St Paul's at Covent Garden. Martin, who was none too sober himself, at first thought the body was that of one of the many celebrants who had chosen the Piazza as a convenient outdoor toilet and dormitory. Being a seasoned Londoner, Martin gave the body the 'London once-over' – a quick glance to determine whether this was a drunk, a crazy or a human being in distress. The fact that it was entirely possible for someone to be all three simultaneously is why good-Samaritanism in London is considered an extreme sport – like base-jumping or crocodile-wrestling. Martin, noting the good-quality coat and shoes, had just pegged the body as a drunk when he noticed that it was in fact missing its head.
>
> As Martin noted to the detectives conducting his interview, it was a good thing he'd been inebriated because otherwise he

would have wasted time screaming and running about – especially once he realised he was standing in a pool of blood. Instead, with the slow, methodical patience of the drunk and terrified, Martin Turner dialled 999 and asked for the police.

The police emergency centre alerted the nearest Incident Response Vehicle and the first officers arrived on the scene six minutes later. One officer stayed with a suddenly sober Martin while his partner confirmed that there was a body and that, everything else being equal, it probably wasn't a case of accidental death. They found the head six metres away where it had rolled behind one of the neoclassical columns that fronted the church's portico. The responding officers reported back to control, who alerted the area Murder Investigation Team whose duty officer, the most junior detective constable on the team, arrived half an hour later: he took one look at Mr Headless and woke his governor. With that, the whole pomp and majesty that is a Metropolitan Police murder investigation descended on the twenty-five metres of open cobbles between the church portico and the market building. The pathologist arrived to certify death, make a preliminary assessment of the cause and cart the body away for its post-mortem. (There was a short delay while they found a big enough evidence bag for the head.) The forensic teams turned up mob-handed and, to prove that they were the important ones, demanded that the secure perimeter be extended to include the whole west end of the Piazza. To do this they needed more uniforms at the scene, so the DCI who was the Senior Investigating Officer called up Charing Cross nick and asked if they had any to spare. The shift commander, upon hearing the magic word 'overtime', marched into the section house and volunteered everyone out of their nice warm beds. Thus the secure perimeter was expanded, searches were made, junior detectives sent off on mysterious errands and finally, at just after five o'clock, it all ground to a halt. The body was gone, the detectives had left and the forensic people unanimously agreed that there was nothing more that could be done until dawn – which was three hours away. Until then, they just needed a couple of mugs to guard the crime scene until shift change.

Which is how I came to be standing around Covent Garden in a freezing wind at six o'clock in the morning, and why it was me that met the ghost.

From *The Rivers of London* by Ben Aaronovitch

This is the opening of Ben Aaronovitch's first novel in his extraordinary police procedural plus ghosties, ghoulies and goddesses crime series. It is worth looking at in some detail, not necessarily because I would advocate trying to write like Aaronovitch – he has a very distinctive and idiosyncratic voice – but because he manages superbly the balancing act between the world we recognize and the world of the paranormal.

Shaping the reader's expectations

Take a few moments now to jot down some notes for yourself about how these four paragraphs work in positioning the reader and shaping their expectations.

The things that strike me most forcefully are the geographical setting, the use of language and the point of view. These three elements will, I believe, be very useful tools to consider making use of when writing your own paranormal crime novel.

Let's take the opening sentence for a start. Here, we are given the precise time, day, month and location, and the name of the first character we encounter. The effect of this is twofold – firstly, it locates us firmly within a known and recognizable world. Even if we are not familiar with January in England, or with this area of central London, we feel that it is a real place, with a real climate and real buildings. Secondly, it sounds slightly bureaucratic, preparing us almost subconsciously for the fact that the narrator is a police officer. Take a moment to think about where your paranormal story will be set, and what details you will give your reader to aid a sense of its substance and reality. Jot down some notes for yourself.

Next, let's look at Aaronovitch's use of language, and at two things in particular that he does very skilfully. Take these three sentences, for instance: 'The <u>forensic teams</u> turned up mob-handed and, to prove that they were the important ones, demanded that the <u>secure perimeter</u> be extended to include the whole west end of the Piazza. To do this they needed more <u>uniforms</u> at the scene, so the <u>DCI</u> who was the <u>Senior Investigating Officer</u> called up <u>Charing Cross nick</u> and asked if they had any to spare. The <u>shift commander</u>, upon hearing the magic word 'overtime', marched into the <u>section house</u> and volunteered everyone out of their nice warm beds.' I have underlined all the 'insider' and specialist terms that Aaronovitch uses, which put us inside the police culture, again providing a sense of familiarity, ease and substance. We are, it seems, securely lodged within the world of the police procedural – at least, until the final sentence of the passage.

Setting narrative tone

Finally, in terms of the elements that I picked out, let's look at the narrative voice. The whole book is told from the point of view of Peter Grant, the young police officer who is soon to learn that he has, if not magic powers, at least magic propensities. We don't in fact know that it is Peter talking (and at this stage we don't know his name or very much else about him) but Aaronovitch has already built up a relationship between the reader and the narrator through the way in which the narrator speaks. He is friendly, chatty, slightly knowing, gently ironic – 'a convenient outdoor toilet and dormitory', 'the "London once-over"', 'why good-Samaritanism in London is considered an extreme sport' – but Aaronovitch also subtly induces a sense of identification and sympathy between the reader and the narrator. The opening sentence of the book establishes that it is very late at night or very early in the morning on a bitterly cold January day. When we learn that the shift commander 'volunteered everyone out of their nice warm beds', we know, without being explicitly told, two things: there was no question of 'volunteering', and it was the narrator who had been in a 'nice warm bed' until roused out to 'maintain the perimeter'. Our sympathies, then, are firmly with Peter as he is left 'standing around Covent Garden in a freezing wind' and we are, as it were, standing shoulder to shoulder with him, trusting, confiding, friendly, when we come to his startling final statement, 'why it was me that met the ghost'. But because we already feel that we know and like Peter, and that he seems reliable and knowledgeable, we don't simply recoil at his statement, but are rather intrigued and engaged. It is less of an 'oh, yeah?' and more of an 'Oh, tell me more' that is elicited from the reader, simply because of the way in which Aaronovitch has built the reality of the scene and the sympathetic trustworthiness of the narrator.

There are, of course, many other ways and tones of voice in which to write paranormal crime fiction, but these three elements of a reality in which we can believe, a world in which we can feel included and a narrator we can trust are commonly crucial to the success of the story.

Establishing the baseline

It is interesting to compare John Connelly's Charlie Parker series to Ben Aaronovitch's London-based paranormal crime stories. Connelly, an Irishman, sets his paranormal stories in America, with Parker, a private investigator, as his central character, with two subsidiary characters in Louis and Angel, a gay couple who are also lethal hitmen and who seem to have some equivocal status not of this world. 'This world' is, of course, the world of the book, but Connelly is also careful to establish it as the world of an America we recognize and feel we know. Above and beyond this world, though, Connelly evokes a world of ghosts and spirits, a world where good and evil exist eternally. And for Charlie Parker, Angel and Louis, sometimes these worlds overlap or collide. But the 'supernatural' only works because there is a baseline of 'natural' against which it plays.

What this means in practice to you as a writer of paranormal crime fiction is that you can be as outlandish as you like in terms of creatures, abilities and actions, so long as you have got your reader safely rooted inside the world of the book – a world that is consistent, familiar and recognizable in some way or another. If you are to carry your reader with you, you must look to provide a sense of normality within which, or more accurately, over and above which the paranormal can function.

How is this to be achieved?

Selecting a setting

The first thing is to choose a setting for your story with which you are very familiar and which you can describe in enough evocative detail to make it real to your reader – this could be where you work, a café you like, your living room . . . Then note down all the details that will give it substance and reality for your reader. The story doesn't have to be confined to this one place, but building the reality of this place will help you with building the reality of the whole world of the book.

As an indication of the kind of thing I have in mind, I will make a start on this exercise myself:

My story will be set in: my study.

The details that I will pick out to make it substantial and real are: the lamp, the fireplace, the beams, the bookshelves.

CORE EXERCISE: METAPHOR AND SIMILE

Simply listing the details is not going to be enough – they are real to me because I can look around myself and see them all, and I already have a whole stack of pictures of them in my head. But how do you get pictures into your readers' heads? How do you make them feel familiar and real? By picking out particular characteristics, particular aspects of your chosen details that will enable your reader to form an image of them for themselves, using comparisons, metaphors and similes that they can relate to. For instance (and this is not an example of good writing, just a suggestion of how you could go about it):

The library lamp, as it was called encouragingly in the catalogue, shone a gentle and forgiving light over my desk. The glass shade, a tint of green I'd only ever seen before on snooker tables, seemed less evocative of libraries than of casinos and smoke-filled bars. Not inappropriate for the lottery that is a writer's day . . .

OK, over to you. I suggest you spend half an hour to an hour on this exercise, writing about 400–500 words. Take it step by step – location, detail, evocation – and make everything as solid and substantial as you can.

Once you've got your 'reality' established, that is, of course, only half the battle. The other half is to evoke a believable and interesting paranormal world that exists within, above or below your 'real' world. Not nearly as easy to do as it is to say. Again, there are some questions you can answer to help you get the balance right:

Why paranormal? What is it about the paranormal world you are evoking which is important to your story?

- Is it to bring out the eternal struggle between the forces of good and evil?
- Is it to suggest that there is a hidden world all around us every day that reflects and informs our actions?
- Is it to comment on the 'normality' of the world you see around you?

Whatever your aims are, you need to be clear about them so that you can deploy the unexpected characters and the unexpected occurrences to achieve the effects that you are seeking. Just to refer back to the two authors we discussed earlier, neither Ben Aaronovitch nor John Connelly fully explain what the paranormal is or how it relates to the everyday world of their books. In fact, in each case, the central character is unsure what is happening, cannot explain it, but accepts what he witnesses however unexpected and unusual. The protagonists' lack of understanding of *how* things are happening together with their acceptance *that* these things are happening make it possible for the reader to suspend their own disbelief and to have their own questions, if not answered, then at least put into abeyance for the duration of the story.

One way in which you may find it helpful to do this is through a deliberate use of metaphor and simile.

So, final questions before you start writing: Who is your protagonist? What is their relationship to the paranormal? How do you want your reader to feel about them? What is the core event of the book? How is the paranormal involved in this? What do you want your reader to be thinking and feeling by the end of your book?

CHAPTER 12
THE HISTORICAL

Author in the Spotlight: Lindsey Davis
Chapter Focus: Dialogue and detail

It is all too easy to make historical fiction sound deadly dull, packed with facts that drag the story down. Lindsey Davis has an extraordinary skill in providing fascinating detail in such a way that it both engages the reader and moves the story on. As you read through the passage below, from *The Silver Pigs*, it's interesting to see not only just how much we learn about life in Rome in the first century AD but also how those details are significant to the story. Have a look out not only for *what* we learn, but also *why* we are being told about it.

We both turned to survey my young lady.

She wore a fine white under tunic fixed along the sleeves with blue enamel clasps, and over it a sleeveless gown so generous in length it was bunched up over her girdle of woven golden threads. Apart from the wide bands of patterned embroidery at her neck, and hem, and in broad stripes down the front, I could tell from the narrowing of Lenia's watery eyes we were admiring a quality cloth. My goddess had wire hoops threaded with tiny glass beads in each neat little ear, a couple of chain necklaces, three bracelets on her left arm, four on her right, and various finger rings in the form of knots, serpents or birds with long crossed beaks. We could have sold her girlish finery for more than I earned last year. It was best not to consider how much a brothel keeper might pay us for the pretty wench.

She was blonde. Well, she was blonde that month, and since she was hardly from Macedonia or Germany, dye must have helped. It was cleverly done. I would never have known, but Lenia informed me afterwards.

Her hair had been curled into three soft fat ringlets tied in a clump with a ribbon at the nape of her neck. The temptation to untie that ribbon niggled me like a hornet bite. She painted her face of course. All my sisters turned themselves out spanking with colour like newly gilt statues, so I was used to that. My sisters are amazing, but blatant works of art. This was much more subtle, invisibly achieved, except that running in the heat had left one eye very faintly smudged. Her eyes were brown, set wide apart, and sweetly without guile.

Lenia tired of looking long before I did.

'Cradle snatcher!' she told me frankly. 'Tinkle in the bucket before you take her up.'

This was not a request for a medical sample because cradle snatching made Lenia diagnose me as unwell; it was a straight hospitable offer, with business overtones.

I shall have to explain about the bucket and the bleach vat.

A long time afterwards I described all this to someone I knew well, and we discussed what launderers use for whitening cloth.

'Distilled woodash?' my companion suggested doubtfully.

They do use ash. They also use carbonate of soda, fuller's earth, and pipeclay for the brilliant robes of election candidates. But the pristine togas of our magnificent Empire are effectively bleached with urine, obtained from the public latrines. The Emperor Vespasian, never slow to light on brisk new ways of squeezing out cash, had slapped a tax on the ancient trade in human waste. Lenia paid the tax, though on principle she increased her supply for nothing whenever she could.

The woman I had been telling the story to commented, in her cool way, 'I suppose in salad season, when everyone's eating beetroot, half the togas in the Forum are a delicate hue of pink? Do they rinse out?' she enquired.

I shrugged in a deliberately vague way. I would have skipped this unsavoury detail but as it turned out eventually, Lenia's bleach vat was critical to the tale.

Since I lived six floors up in a block that was no better equipped than any other slum in Rome, Lenia's bucket had long been my welcome friend.

From *The Silver Pigs* by Lindsey Davis

There is a great skill to writing historical crime fiction, and perhaps none are more skilful than Lindsey Davis in her Falco series. There are two yawning potential pitfalls for those writing historical fiction, both of which Davis evades with misleading ease. The first is the question of detail; the other is the question of language.

Deploying details

In order to be both convincing and engaging, the writer has to know a great deal about their subject – just as with the crime-fiction genres we looked at in Part 2: Taking You Behind the Scenes, you must have done a lot of research in order to be able to share the right information with your reader in the right way. The trick that Lindsey Davis uses is to write as if taking everything for granted – this is the world that the characters inhabit and it is not strange to them – while at the same time giving plausible reasons for explaining things that are inherently interesting and that need explaining in order for the story to work.

It's worth looking at this passage from the first of the Falco book series, *The Silver Pigs*, in a little detail in order to see just what it is that Davis does, and how she does it. First of all, let's take the historical details of Vespasian's Rome, which may be unfamiliar to the reader, and which provide texture and substance to the story – hair-dying, make-up and the exploitation of urine. Each of the details brings the reader back to the Roman world – Falco (or rather Lenia) knows that the young girl has bleached her hair because she's Roman, not a natural blonde from Macedonia or Germany. He knows that she is wearing make-up because he has seen his sisters wearing it. Finally, we learn a great deal about the sewage disposal methods of ancient Rome through Falco's discussion of the vat of urine. Lenia is a laundress and uses urine to help bleach the white linen in which the Roman nobility are dressed. But we gather much more information in this brief passage – being on the sixth floor of the tenement block in which he lives, Falco has no lavatory so Lenia's vat is a convenient alternative to the public latrines. We even get a hint of Emperor Vespasian's character in his thrifty imposition of a tax on the use of urine . . . A lot of the everyday details of life in ancient Rome are slipped in here almost invisibly.

Playing with language

The second potential pitfall for the unwary writer of historical crime fiction is what to do about the language. In fact, more accurately, there are two pitfalls. All too often, a writer can find themselves using the language of the time about which they're writing in such a way that, to our modern ears, it sounds false and stilted. On the other side of this delicate equation is the use of anachronistic language. Using language that is too contemporary can jar with the reader and detract from the sense of 'being taken away from the world we know' by bringing us back into the modern day with an unpleasant bump.

Lindsey Davis's solution to these twin puzzles is to write pretty much consistently in contemporary British English, using the Roman terms where they are inescapable – when dealing with social ranks, for instance – but sticking as far as possible to the tone and vocabulary that would have been used by her characters in their native language. This is part of what gives Davis's writing its liveliness and zest.

In terms of your own writing, the first decision you need to make is, what period of history are you going to be writing about? And what is it about that period of history that will be interesting for your readers?

• The social changes taking place?
• The technology?
• The beliefs?
• The values?

The answers to these questions lead naturally on to the second set of decisions you will need to make. Who are your characters? What social class do they inhabit? What challenges face them?

The answers to these questions will give you the broad outline of where and when your book is going to be set and what kind of lives your characters are going to be leading. Two further choices follow on from this. The first is, what is the crime? Is it a crime distinctive to that period of history? If so, how and why? The second question, once you have all these elements settled in your mind, is how much research are you going to need to do, and how are you going to go about it?

Getting the voices right

Once you're happy and settled with all these elements of your story, you are eventually going to have to start writing . . . And this is where the great challenge for the historical novelist comes to the fore – how are your characters going to talk to each other?

The question of dialogue is often a vexatious one for the writer. No matter the kind of fiction we are writing, it is all too easy to make our characters sound stilted, wooden and unconvincing. There are various ways of avoiding this, as we shall see in a minute, but essentially there is one important point that you need to settle in your mind in terms of your own characters, and that is, what are you using dialogue for?

There are two main reasons for using dialogue in fiction: to provide your characters with distinctive voices that give an insight into what they are like and how we, as readers, should relate to them; and, secondly, to move the story along. The moving the story along bit can often be slightly tricky if we haven't got the distinctive voices bit sorted out first. It's all too easy to fall into giving your characters lines like, 'Oh, look, is that a sinister-looking man in a dark cape lurking behind that wall?' – a sentence that may help the reader know what's going on in terms of plot, but also a sentence that, I'd be prepared to wager, would never be spoken in actual conversation by anyone, anywhere, at any time.

I am exaggerating, of course, but you take my point. The trick, then, is to establish, first of all in your head and then on the page, just how your characters will speak, given the time about which you are writing, their social class, their level of education, their personality and all the other factors that make up their distinctive voices.

As mentioned earlier, we are extraordinarily lucky, as writers in English, in that we have a whole range of different languages at our fingertips, and which immediately signal a great deal about social class and attitude. For historical reasons – and, of course, as writers of historical crime fiction, this is something of which you can make full use – we have two main lexicons on which to draw: the Anglo-Saxon lexicon, with its Germanic roots and its connotations of direct conversational speech, which is practical and action-oriented; and then we also have the French/Norman/Latin lexicon, with its connotations of power, authority, education and obfuscation. Added to this, of course, come all the heterogeneous words borrowed down the ages from peoples whose lands we have invaded or who have immigrated to this country. And finally, there is the ever-changing swirling sea of slang that ebbs and flows in our speech, marking us out in terms of age and social grouping. A word of warning, though – nothing dates faster than slang, so, unless you're using it for deliberate effect, it is a linguistic spice to be used exceedingly sparingly.

CORE EXERCISE: GIVING VOICE

The fact that we have all these different kinds of vocabulary that we can deploy in so many different ways provides the writing of historical fiction with an extraordinarily rich toolbox, since a lot can be conveyed to the reader simply by using these different lexicons in different ways for your different characters. Here is a brief exercise for you to play with, which will give you a sense of how you might use these different vocabularies in your own writing.

Imagine that Robin Hood has been brought before the Sheriff of Nottingham. Robin Hood is an Anglo-Saxon noble and is determined only to speak in words with Anglo-Saxon roots. The Sheriff, being French-Norman, could never bring himself to say anything that does not have a French/Norman/Latin word at its root. Write a dialogue between them, discussing Robin's commitment to easing the plight of the peasants whose lives have been overturned by the oppressive nature of King John's rule. It's a fairly tough exercise so I don't suggest more than 200–300 hundred words. Once it's done, have a look at the different characters and points of view expressed by the two men in the language you have given them to use. How do you think you might apply this in your own writing?

CHAPTER 13
EXOTIC LOCATIONS

Author in the Spotlight: Donna Leon
Chapter Focus: Place as character

This passage is from early on in Donna Leon's *Beastly Things* and shows very clearly how Leon has integrated place, personality and plot in her books about the Venice police. As you read through, look for all the elements that make this setting uniquely Venetian. How does that impact the plot?

'You don't walk around with a knife that long unless you have a reason to. You have to think about how to carry it so no one will see it.'

'And that suggests premeditation?'

'I think so. He wasn't killed in the kitchen or the workshop or wherever else a knife might be lying around, was he?'

Bocchese shrugged.

'What does that mean?' Brunetti asked, leaning one hip against the desk and folding his arms.

'We don't know where it happened. The ambulance report says he was found in Rio del Malpaga, just behind the Giustinian. Rizzardi says he had water in his lungs, so he could have been killed anywhere and put in the water, then drifted there.' [...]

'It's not an easy thing to do,' Brunetti said.

'What?'

'Slip a body into a canal.'

'From a boat, it might be easier,' Bocchese suggested.

'Then you've got blood in a boat.'

'Fish bleed.'

'And fishing boats have motors, and no motors are allowed after eight at night.'

'Taxis are,' Bocchese volunteered.

'People don't hire taxis to dump bodies in the water,' Brunetti said, familiar with Bocchese's manner.

After only a second hesitation, the technician said, 'Then a boat without a motor.'

'Or a water door from a house.'

'And no nosey neighbours.'

'A quiet canal, a place where there are no neighbours, nosey or otherwise,' Brunetti suggested, starting to examine the map in his head. Then he said, 'Rizzardi's guess was after midnight.'

'Cautious man, the Doctor.'

'Found at six,' Brunetti said.

'"After midnight".' Bocchese said. 'Doesn't mean he went in at midnight.'

'Where behind the Giustinian was he found?' Brunetti asked, needing the first coordinate on his map.

'At the end of Calle Degolin.'

Brunetti made a noise of acknowledgement, glanced at the wall behind Bocchese, and sent himself walking in an impossible circular path, radiating out from that fixed point, jumping over canals from one dead-end *calle* to another, trying, but failing, to recall the buildings that had doors and steps down to the water.

After a moment, Bocchese said, 'Better asked Foa about the tides. He'd know.'

It had been Brunetti's thought as well.

From *Beastly Things* by Donna Leon

Crime fiction set in exotic locations is becoming an increasingly well-recognized genre. For our purposes here, in terms of developing our own writing strategies and style, crime fiction set in exotic locations is taken to refer to novels set in locations that are exotic to the writer, rather than crime fiction in translation. There is a reason for this. Locations that may seem exotic to the reader – Alaska, Botswana, Norway, Sweden and Denmark to name but a few that have given birth to superb crime-fiction writing – are sometimes ingrained in a native writer's day-to-day experience, and although the locations may well be highly significant in the way in which their stories unfold, they are also, to some extent, a given. Here I would rather look at how to use location as a shaping force in the narrative – effectively as an additional character. To do this I have selected as our exemplar one of the supreme virtuosos of this genre, and that is Donna Leon, with her stories set in Venice. Although Leon has lived in Venice for a number of years, she still, as an American, comes to the city with fresh eyes and with a fascination for the way in which things work (or don't). Nothing is taken for granted, every detail is relished and every aspect of the place is made integral to the story.

In the passage quoted above, a body has just been found in one of Venice's quieter canals, and Inspector Brunetti and one of his team are trying to work out from where it might have come. This is a superb example of the way Donna Leon makes the setting for her Brunetti books an integral and indispensable part of the plot. The complexities of the interwoven web of canals and side streets, the question of where and how the murderer could have accessed the water, the ebb and flow of the tides, all of these are central to how the story is going to unfold. All of which is to say, whatever the exotic location in which you choose to set your novel, it is important to make the location a significant part of the story, rather than simply a backdrop for the action.

Focusing on special places

As well as being a significant part of the story, the location must also be sufficiently distinctive and unusual to engage the reader's interest. Without in any way wishing to malign Bognor or Balham, they probably don't have the fascination of the unknown and the exotic of, say, Banff or Bangalore. But just being far away is not enough – there must be something about the place in which you have chosen to set your story that makes it different from all other places, in its geography, in its climate, in its culture . . . something that will make the reader feel that they are being taken to somewhere new and unknown, even if it's a place that they may have visited.

Some questions that may help you decide where to set your story are:

1. Where is the place you have in mind?
2. What makes it distinctive?
3. What is the climate like?
4. How easy/hard is it to get to?

Linking the crime

Now have a think about what kind of crime would be best set in this place:

* Will it be linked to the geography of the location you have in mind? Very hot? Very cold? Very wet? Very dry?
* Will it be tied to the culture of the place? Religious practices? Beliefs? Taboos?
* Will it arise from the economy of the place? Gold mining? Fishing? Logging?
* Will it draw on the history of the place? Ruins? Buried treasure? Archaeological finds?

Research, research, research

You have the location of your story; you have the crime that will form the pivot of the action; now how are you going to bring it all to life in the mind of your reader? As with many of the other kinds of crime fiction we've been looking at, the iceberg principle applies here too – you are going to need to know a lot more than you ever communicate to your reader, but the details that you select, and the manner in which you convey them, will make all the difference in terms of taking your reader to a location that they will engage with and believe in.

Research inevitably plays its part here and, although online searches and satellite maps can be enormously helpful, there really is no substitute for going to the location you're going to write about, ideally more than once, and making copious notes of everything that you see, smell, hear and otherwise experience. The upside of this, of course, is that, if you play your cards right, your three weeks in Marrakesh could become a tax-deductible expense . . .

Assume, then, you have done all your research, and that you know precisely the character and geography of the place you're going to be writing about – how are you going to convey that to the reader in a way that adds to the story and doesn't make you sound like a travel agent's brochure?

Fundamentally, this is a question of selection – the gathering together of small details that will evoke being in this place through all the senses, in just the same way that you experienced it when you were there.

To help you do this, here is a checklist of the kind of details you may want to have at your fingertips so that you can bring them into your story at the appropriate time and build up a solid sense of place in your reader's mind.

CORE EXERCISE: CREATING PLACE

1. Usual weather prevailing
2. Unusual weather that might occur

3. From what are houses made?
4. From what are government buildings made?
5. From what are office buildings made?
6. What do people usually eat every day?
7. What do people eat on special occasions?
8. Usual drinks
9. Unusual drinks
10. Spices used
11. Market places and shops – what do they sell?
12. Streets and roads – what are they made of? Are they well maintained?
13. What are the prevailing sights?
14. What are the prevailing smells?
15. Anything else at all . . .

One last final point before you set off on your own writing – don't be tempted to cut corners. If you don't know how your character can get from the corner café to the nearest supermarket, don't make it up and don't guess. Either research it yourself when you're there, in the flesh, or build a relationship with a local who can check these things out for you as they arise. Parking regulations, one-way systems, all can change in the blink of an eye, and a satellite map will only give you a partial and dated view. It's worth being scrupulous over these details – nothing is going to lose your reader's respect more quickly than the inclusion of an event or a location that they know to be wrong.

And now, enjoy your research, enjoy your planning and, above all, enjoy your writing.

PART 4:
THE LONG, THE SHORT AND THE RATHER TALL STORY

TECHNICAL FOCUS: FOCUS AND SELECTION

CHAPTER 14
TRUE CRIME

Author in the Spotlight: David Smith
Chapter Focus: Telling details

True crime treads a delicate line between information and intrusion – we are almost all fascinated by just how and why human beings behave as they do in extreme situations, whether for good or ill – but it is all too easy to tip over from curiosity into a kind of pornography. This passage, from David Smith's autobiographical account of his experience of the murderous outrages committed by Ian Brady and Myra Hindley, wavers around that line without ever quite stumbling across it. There are at least two different kinds of narrative technique used in this passage, which guide the reader's responses so that they get a sense of what Smith has seen and how he has reacted to what he has seen. Where in the passage does the narrative technique change, and why?

Forgive me, Father (and that eternal fucking mother thing). It's been too many years since I made my last confession.

I am forever a Catholic, an illegitimate stink off the cobbled streets of Manchester, brought up correctly by a deformed old woman whom I adored. As a child, I was happy with my religion, saying my prayers just like good boys do, thanking You for everything – good and bad – and I really did believe that life itself was governed by Your will.

And then You turned away . . .

You turned away. Couldn't You face my questions? Couldn't You face Your answers? All the crap I was brought up on – when

I needed my faith, You took it away and disappeared. You left me with nothing. I was surrounded by blood, shit and spilt brains, and what did You do?

You left me to choke on it.

Inside I was screaming. Why couldn't You hear my silence? Why couldn't You see I was falling apart? You left me hanging off the end of a fucking rosary instead.

Fucking cunt, dirty bastard . . . In a nice, normal overspill living room Ian is killing a lad with an axe, repeating those same words over and over again. The lad is lying with his head and shoulders on the settee, his legs sprawled on the floor, facing upwards. Ian stands over him, legs on either side of the screaming lad. The television is the only light in the room.

The lad falls onto the floor, onto his stomach, still screaming. Ian keeps hitting him; even when the lad falls beneath the table, Ian goes after him, drags him out and hits him again. He swings the axe and it grazes the top of Myra's head. There is blood everywhere. Then he stops and shouts: *get the fucking dogs away from the blood, get the fucking things out of it . . .*

The lad is lying on his face, feet near the door. Ian kneels down and strangles him, pulling something tight around his throat. The lad's head is destroyed already; he rattles and gurgles, a thick, wet sound, a low sound. Then lower: more effort from Ian, and lower, and lower, then nothing but silence, everlasting silence.

Ian stands, breathing heavily, but casually looking at his hands, drenched in blood. His voice is blunt as he speaks to Myra: *that's it, the messiest one yet . . .*

> From *Evil Relations: The Man Who Bore Witness Against the Moors Murderers* by David Smith with Carol Ann Lee

This passage comes from a book partly written by David Smith, Myra Hindley's ex-brother-in-law and the main prosecution witness at the Moors Murderers' trial. Smith also had a ghostwriter to help him narrate and structure the story. Smith was seventeen years old at the time of the events described in this passage.

This particular excerpt is from Smith's own memoirs, quotations from which are interspersed throughout the book. The structure of the book as a whole is interesting from this point of view. The majority of the narrative is third person, but written from Smith's point of view, though with the benefit of hindsight and with a lot of time having passed between the writing and the events described (*Evil Relations* was first published in 2011, Brady and Hindley were tried and found guilty of murder in 1966).

Why true crime?

There is no doubt that true crime is a highly popular genre, as readers try to come to grips with the baffling question of just how criminals think. What is it in their minds or in their make-up that makes them able to step over the line into cruel, violent, self-serving behaviour? Are they in some way different from the rest of us? Or are we potentially just like them?

Narrating factual events, rather than making up fictional ones, presents its own particular set of problems, accuracy not being the least among them. Your research needs to be done thoroughly and meticulously, and there are many books, courses and mentors who can guide you through that process. What I would like to focus on here, though, are the choices available to you as a writer. Almost always you will be describing events at which you were not present, taking the accounts of others and weaving them into a narrative of your own. But even if you were present, as David Smith was at the murder of Edward Evans, telling the story of the event inevitably involves choices and compromises. It is impossible to narrate every detail of even a single moment of experience – novelists have tried again and again, with very limited success. Our consciousness is too complex, our language too limited, the time frames too radically different – what takes an instant to see may take whole pages to tell. Fundamentally, the whole way in which narrative functions has to be by selecting and shaping.

Changing the narrative

If we look a little at the extract from Smith's memoir with which we opened this chapter, it becomes clear that various things are happening in the language that reveal the turbulence of his feelings, and the difficulty he has, in the narrative, of presenting the lived experience.

There are three voices and two time-schemes functioning in this passage. In terms of voices, there is the David who is writing, the David who is present at the murder at the time and Ian Brady's dialogue, while the time slides from the **past historic** to the **narrative present**. So what does this mean in terms of what the writer is expressing, and what the reader experiences? And what can we, as writers, learn?

In the opening paragraphs of the passage, David Smith is writing looking back on this pivotal event and berating the God in whom he was brought up to believe for apparently abandoning him when he most needed His help. The anger in these opening paragraphs is easily apparent, through the deliberately shocking language – 'that eternal fucking mother thing', 'All the crap I was brought up on', 'You left me hanging off the end of a fucking rosary' – but perhaps even more through the short sentences and the repeated questions. Suddenly, though, and with a highly disorienting effect for the reader, we are no longer looking back on the traumatic murder of Edward Evans; we are there in the room as it happens, in the present tense. Although there is a deep sense of shock, there is also a real feeling of dissociation. The heightened language and vivid detail ('I was surrounded by blood, shit and spilt brains') of the earlier paragraphs is left behind to be replaced by a factual, detached, unemotional setting down of the events as they occur, without comment. This happens, then that happens, then that happens . . . The young man, Edward Evans, is nameless – 'the lad'. Some of the few **adjectives** used occur in the very opening of this passage, where Smith describes the setting for these events – 'a nice, normal overspill living room' – in a way that heightens the sense of disbelief and dissociation. The **adverbs** used – 'breathing heavily', 'casually looking at his hands' – again reinforce the ordinariness of Brady's attitude in contrast to his actions.

Approaching true crime

We have looked at this passage in detail because it highlights very usefully the major questions that a writer of true-life crime must address. Essentially, these are as follows.

Why this crime?

Why is this crime, among all the other crimes, sufficiently interesting and significant to write about? There could be a range of answers to this – it was particularly horrific; it was hard to solve; it involved a great number of people, or continued over a great length of time; it required outstanding forensic skill to bring the perpetrator to trial . . . For David Smith the choice was straightforward – the crime took place in front of his eyes and totally altered the direction of his life. Note down the crime, or crimes, you'd be interested in writing about, and why you think it, or they, are interesting and significant.

What should the reader feel and understand?

What do you want your reader to feel when reading your account of what happened? This, of course, is closely related to your answer to the previous question but with a slightly different emphasis. The first question was concerned with the 'what' of the crime, so to speak – what makes it stand out? What makes it interesting? This question, though, relates more to the 'why' – why do we care about what happened? Why do you want to share these events, and your understanding and feelings about them, with your readers? How do you want your readers to be affected, and why?

What research is needed?

What do you need to know in order to tell the story of the crime or crimes effectively? What research do you need to do? Where will you find the information you need? What do you need to do in order to access it? For instance, will you be researching contemporary accounts – newspapers, video clips and so on? Will you be interviewing people involved? If so, who and how? And why should they talk to you?

Once you have the answers to these three questions, you're ready to start writing. Before you do, though, select a scene from the story you're about to tell and try out the following exercise.

CORE EXERCISE: TELLING DETAILS

1. Draft a broad overview of the scene about which you're going to write, simply noting down, in bullet-point form if you find that easiest, who was there and what happened.
2. Take each element that you've noted down and add as much detail as you can – what the actors were wearing, what the weather was like, whether there were any neighbours . . . whatever is going to bring the scene to life in the mind of your reader and give it substance and a sense of reality.
3. Lastly, against each of these details, give a clear account of *how* you know this. Court records? Police statements? Newspaper account?

When writing about true crime, you're essentially being a historian and you need to establish clearly for your reader what is known as fact, what is held as opinion and, finally, what is essentially your own point of view or your interpretation of events.

Now write your scene in detail, giving clear guidance to your reader as to what you know happened, what might have happened and what you think about what happened.

Done with care, and respect for the facts and for your reader, it is a fascinating area to explore.

CHAPTER 15
FICTIONALIZED TRUE CRIME

Author in the Spotlight: Truman Capote
Chapter Focus: Selection

In this passage, taken from about two-thirds of the way through Truman Capote's *In Cold Blood*, Capote is telling the story of the policeman, Dewey, after he has apprehended one of the killers, questioning him about what happened on the night of the killings. What effect does it have on the reader to have Dewey's imagined responses to what he is hearing?

'Wait. I'm not telling it the way it was.' Perry scowls. He rubs his legs; the handcuffs rattle. 'After, see, after we'd taped them, Dick and I went off in a corner. To talk it over. Remember, now, there were hard feelings between us. Just then it made my stomach turn to think I'd ever admired him, lapped up all that brag. I said, "Well, Dick. Any qualms?" He didn't answer me. I said, "Leave them alive, and this won't be any small rap. Ten years the very least." He still didn't say anything. He was still holding the knife. I asked him for it, and he gave it to me, and I said, "All right, Dick. Here goes." But I didn't mean it. I meant to call his bluff, make him argue me out of it, make him admit he was a phoney and a coward. See, it was something between me and Dick. I knelt down beside Mr. Clutter, and the pain of kneeling – I thought of that goddam dollar. Silver dollar. The shame. Disgust. And *they'd* told me never to come back to Kansas. But I didn't realise what I'd done till I heard the sound. Like somebody drowning. Screaming under water. I handed the knife to Dick. I said, "Finish him. You'll feel better." Dick tried – or pretended to. But the man had the strength of ten men – he was half out of his ropes, his hands were free. Dick panicked. Dick wanted to get the hell out of there. But I wouldn't let him go. The man would have died anyway, I know that, but I couldn't leave him like he was. I told Dick to hold the flashlight, focus it. Then I aimed the gun. The room just exploded. Went blue. Just blazed up. Jesus, I'll never understand why they didn't hear the noise twenty miles around.'

Dewey's ears rang with it – a ringing that almost deafens him to the whispery rush of Smith's soft voice. But the voice plunges on, ejecting a fusillade of sounds and images . . . Hickock hunting the discharged shell; hurrying, hurrying, and Kenyon's head in a circle of light, the murmur of muffled pleadings, then Hickock again scrambling after a used cartridge; Nancy's room, Nancy listening to boots on hardwood stairs, the creak of the steps as they climb towards her, Nancy's eyes, Nancy watching the flashlight's shine seek the target ('She said, "Oh, no! Oh, please. No! No! No! No! Don't! Oh, please don't! Please!" I gave the gun to Dick. I told him I'd done all I could do. He took aim, and she turned her face to the wall'); the dark hall, the assassins hastening towards the final door. Perhaps, having heard all she had, Bonnie welcomed their swift approach . . .

A hush. For ten miles and more, the three men ride without speaking.

Sorrow and profound fatigue are at the heart of Dewey's silence. It had been his ambition to learn 'exactly what happened in that house that night.' Twice now he'd been told, and the two versions were very much alike, the only serious discrepancy being that Hickock attributed all four deaths to Smith, while Smith contended that Hickock had killed the two women. But the confessions, though they answered questions of how and why, failed to satisfy his sense of meaningful design. The crime was a psychological accident, virtually an impersonal act; the victims might as well have been killed by lightning. Except for one thing: they had experienced prolonged terror, they had suffered. And Dewey could not forget their sufferings. Nonetheless, he found it possible to look at the man beside him without anger – with, rather, a measure of sympathy – for Perry's life had been no bed of roses, but pitiful, an ugly and lonely progress toward one mirage and then another. Dewey's sympathy, however, was not deep enough to accommodate either forgiveness or mercy. He hoped to see Perry and his partner hanged back to back.

Duntz asks Smith, 'Added up, how much money did you get from the Clutters?'

'Between forty and fifty dollars.'

From *In Cold Blood* by Truman Capote

In Cold Blood is a strange and fascinating book. It gives all the appearance of being a factual narrative of the appalling and arbitrary murder of the Clutter family in 1959. It is, to be sure, very tightly tied to the events and Capote himself claimed that it was non-fiction. There has been a lot of debate, however, pretty much from the moment the book was published, as to the fundamental accuracy of Capote's account and questions as to whether this or that detail did in fact take place in that way at that time. Whatever Capote's own claims that the book is 'scrupulously factual', there is perhaps a more helpful perspective to be gained by considering what Capote himself said he wanted to achieve in the book:

This book was an important event for me. While writing it, I realized I just might have found a solution to what had always been my greatest creative quandary. I wanted to produce a journalistic novel, something on a large scale that would have the credibility of fact, the immediacy of film, the depth and freedom of prose, and the precision of poetry.

No small ambition, but certainly something Capote could be said to have achieved, particularly if we take note of the 'credibility of fact' – something arguably quite different from fact itself.

So how, in this extract from *In Cold Blood*, does Capote create this sense of credibility, immediacy, depth and precision, and what can we learn from his technique that could be applied to our own writing in this genre?

Creating credibility

In this extract, one of the killers is being transported in a police car, together with the senior investigating officer, Dewey, and his junior colleague, Duntz. As they drive along, Perry, the killer, tells his version of the murders. Through the use of dialogue and the apparent replication of Perry's way of speaking – 'Just then it made my stomach turn to think I'd ever admired him, lapped up all that brag' – the reader feels as if they are in the car with the three men, overhearing the conversation. And if you seem to be overhearing a first-hand account, then that cannot but lend it a sense of credibility.

Instilling a sense of immediacy

Again, a sense of immediacy is partly created by the use of dialogue and by the reader's sense of being in this small, contained space with the three men. It is also greatly heightened by Capote's moving between the past historic, in Perry's account of what took place, and the narrative present, in the narrator's description of the thoughts and feelings of the men in the car: 'Sorrow and profound fatigue are at the heart of Dewey's silence.'

In this way Capote has the reader with Perry and Dick as the murders are committed, and with Dewey as he hears the account of the killings. By interweaving the two narratives, and the two time frames, we are privy to Perry's thoughts and feelings while the killings took place and to the lawman's private reactions to the killer's narrative.

Providing depth

The depth, the sense of an examination of the significance and meaning of these events, is provided partly by the narrator's presentation of Dewey's thoughts, which gives the reader the perspective of an experienced and thoughtful law enforcement officer. Capote attributes to Dewey a desire for 'meaningful design' – a desire thwarted by the apparent randomness with which the killings took place: 'The crime was a psychological accident, virtually an impersonal act; the victims might as well have been killed by lightning.' Although apparently part of Dewey's reactions to Perry's confession, this sentence sounds much more like the narrator's own voice and thoughts. This slipping between a journalistic account and an editorial commentary shaping the reader's reactions can be seen either as part of Capote's great skill as the writer of a 'journalistic novel' or as evidence of his bad faith as a recorder of fact – each view has its passionate supporters.

Seeking precision

Capote speaks of seeking the 'precision of poetry' and, indeed, there are a number of very powerful moments that catch the reader's imagination in this passage. Whether they provide the 'precision of poetry' is a moot point, but they certainly give the reader some powerful images that carry us right into the core of what is being described.

There is, for instance, the description of Perry cutting Mr Clutter's throat: 'I knelt down beside Mr. Clutter . . . But I didn't realise what I'd done till I heard the sound. Like somebody drowning. Screaming under water.' Whether the image comes from the killer or from Capote, the effect is extraordinarily potent.

Later on in the passage, there is a pair of sentences that seem to be suspended in time and are ascribed to none of the individuals in the car: 'the dark hall, the assassins hastening towards the final door. Perhaps, having heard all she had, Bonnie welcomed their swift approach . . .' This sudden move into the position of the omniscient narrator gives us a different perspective on the events that took place and on the emotional reaction of the killers' final victim.

What do you want to achieve?

Writing fictionalized true crime is a very powerful way of presenting and examining some of the most extreme events in human experience but it is also fraught with pitfalls. Some of what one human being can do to another is so difficult to believe and, happily, so alien to the majority of us that it is easy to do the written equivalent of those who slow down on the motorway to gaze at traffic accidents – and sometimes cause accidents in their turn.

It is helpful – here perhaps more than in any other genre – to know why it is you have chosen this subject and what it is you want to convey to the reader. Capote, in *In Cold Blood*, was conveying, among other things, his sad bafflement at the random and haphazard nature of the violence he describes.

So what is it you wish to convey? Once you are clear on that, how you convey it will fall much more easily into place.

CORE EXERCISE: SHAPING THE NARRATIVE

Once you're clear on what it is you want your readers to feel and understand, settling how you're going to deal with the following three key elements of your writing technique will help ensure you create the effects you're looking for:

1. Chronology: how are you setting your story in terms of tense?

a. Narrative present? This gives it immediacy but a narrow(ish) perspective.

b. Past historic? This gives it distance and control but risks a loss of immediacy.

c. A mixture of the two? This is what Capote opted for. Would it work for you?

2. Point of view: the viewpoint you adopt will have an enormous impact on how the reader views events so which perspective do you choose?

a. The perpetrator? Getting inside the criminal's mind and seeing actions and events from their point of view.

b. The victim? Bringing out the horror and pathos of the events described.

c. An omniscient narrator? Telling the story in such a way that you can provide everyone's point of view – including your own.

3. The narrator's role: how far are you going to be a commentator on the events you describe?

a. Are you going to be an invisible storyteller, simply describing the events as they unfold and leaving your reader to draw their own conclusions?

b. Are you going to take more of an editorial role, providing a context within which your reader can understand what is going on?

c. Are you going to combine both positions?

Now, with all those elements clear in your mind, it's time to get writing.

CHAPTER 16
THE SHORT STORY

Author in the Spotlight: David Hewson
Chapter Focus: Narrow beam

A short story has to convey a lot of information to the reader in a very limited time. It's worth taking a moment to note down just how much information David Hewson has given us about Alf, his main protagonist, in these seven short paragraphs. What do we know by the end of this passage and what kind of thing do we expect to happen?

When he finally got out of the Scrubs, Eileen had taken matters into her own hands. The terraced house in Plaistow, the place he'd grown up, was gone, she told him as they stood on the prison steps, Alf with his duffel bag in his hand, blinking at the bright July sun. Then she mumbled something that sounded like 'Sleazyjet' and pushed him into a minicab to Gatwick where they flew down to Spain in what appeared to be an orange bus with wings.

Her mum had died not long before his twelve years were up. She'd owned a decrepit pile near the waterfront in Whitstable. While Alf was in jail, trying to teach his cellmate Norm the Chisel that there were better ways to spell 'ink-arse'erashun', it seemed the place had turned from Hoxton by Sea to Islington-sur-Mer. Eileen had sold the dump to a TV producer with funny glasses and a stupid haircut. Best part of a quarter of a million for dry rot, fungal damp and four squawky cats.

Now *that* was robbery, Alf observed mid-flight only to get a whack round the chops in return.

Their new home, a place that 'would keep him out of any more of that trouble he liked so much', was a tiny villa not far from the last motorway turnoff for Fuengirola. Two and a half bedrooms, a patio with a weedy palm tree, a table for drinks with their new-found friends. Who weren't really friends, not to his way of thinking, and tended to show that after a couple of glasses of industrial strength Larios and tonic. Especially after he put up a sign outside the front door that read 'Dunblaggin'.

Irony, he said when she started kicking up a fuss. There'd been a lot of that about since the men from the Yard came a-knocking in the night.

He was sixty-three now, a big bloke, still muscular, all his own teeth, good for something better than hanging round the Costa Del Sol and listening to Radio 2 off their weird iPad thing she'd bought. Bald as a coot, he'd turned walnut after two weeks of Spanish sun. That was the first time he'd looked at himself and thought: you're getting old. Time's running out. And there's still a nasty black mark on your life you never deserved.

From *Last Exit to Fuengirola* by David Hewson

A short story is a different sort of beast from a novel. It is, if you like, sushi to the novel's beef stew. The stew has all sorts of ingredients carefully combined and cooked together to provide a rich intermeshing of flavours and textures; the sushi has a very limited set of ingredients, carefully arranged to provide one single, powerful taste experience. In the same way, a novel can have plots and **subplots**, characters, imagery and events, all carefully interwoven so that sometimes one of them comes to the fore, and sometimes another, but all held together within an imaginative whole. A short story, though, tends to be much more concentrated – a limited set of characters and one central event towards which everything is leading.

The passage quoted above comes from the stylish and effective short story, *Last Exit to Fuengirola*. In it, Hewson tells the story of an ageing man who has spent twelve years in Wormwood Scrubs, a category B prison in central London. His wife, in order, it is implied, to keep him from falling back into former criminal ways, has sold their house in Plaistow and they are now living on the Costa del Sol.

That is what appears to be happening, although there is a hint in the final sentence of the passage quoted that all is not as it seems. There is, says Alf in the interior monologue in which the story is told, 'a nasty black mark on your life you never deserved'.

If there is one thing that is the key to a successful short story, then it is this: to raise a question in the reader's mind within your first three of four paragraphs which will then, gradually or suddenly, be answered in the rest of the story.

You don't have a lot of time to involve your reader in your story, so you need to begin telling the story as close to the end as possible. Although there are no hard and fast rules, it is fair to say that this aspect of the chronology of the narrative is one of the things that mark the short story apart from the novel. In a novel the 'inciting incident' that sets the action rolling usually occurs in the first two or three chapters. In the short story, that incident often took place long before the story starts – the short story, as it were, deals with the aftermath of the incident and its resolution.

If we look for a moment at how David Hewson's story is structured, we can begin to choose how we might like to borrow, adapt or deviate from that structure for our own purposes.

NB: Spoiler alert – if you prefer to read the story in full before looking at how it works here, now's the time to do it!

What happened before the story starts?

In David Hewson's story, we gradually learn that Alf was a police officer who had been framed by a corrupt colleague. That is why he spent twelve years in the Scrubs and why he says there was 'a nasty black mark' on his life that he didn't deserve. The reader only learns this bit by bit, so that they have to piece together the story for themselves until the final confrontation between Alf and his nemesis, when the whole picture is finally put in place.

What triggers the dénouement?

For Alf, the story, and the wiping out of his 'black mark', comes with the discovery that his corrupt colleague is living the life of Riley just a few miles away on the Costa del Sol, still involved in various criminal activities and wanted by a variety of law-enforcement organizations. With the help of friends, Alf apprehends his erstwhile colleague, redeems his reputation and recovers his 'glint'.

What's the story about?

As discussed in Chapter 2, there is fundamental difference between plot and theme.

The plot of Hewson's story is pretty much as described in the previous section. The theme, though, is a much subtler thing and revolves around trust, fidelity, loyalty and belief – it is these qualities that both Alf and Eileen have demonstrated, with regard to their roles in life and in relation to each other, and these are the qualities that are rewarded and vindicated at the end of the story.

So what about your story? Perhaps more than any other form of crime-fiction writing, the short story requires careful planning from the start. The prompts and questions that follow are designed to help you keep everything together and to stay consistently in focus when you start writing.

CORE EXERCISE: STAYING IN FOCUS

1. What is the theme of your story? Loyalty, love, betrayal, belief, trust . . . ?
2. What is the crime that your story hinges on?
3. What is the plot of your story? What are the events you are describing?
4. When does your story start? How much of the plot has taken place before your story opens?
5. What question or questions do you want your reader to ask themselves when your story opens?
6. What resolution do you want them to have reached when your story ends?

Once you've got clarity on these half-dozen points, your story will (almost) write itself. Good luck!

GLOSSARY

Adjective: In purely grammatical terms, a word that describes a noun. For the writer, an adjective is, just like its dynamic little cousin the adverb, both a friend, a temptation and, on occasions, something akin to a drug . . . Adjectives provide colour and substance to whatever you are writing about but they can also slow down the pace of the text and, on occasions, overload the reader with information. It's worth being quite stern with your adjectives and checking that each one is actually adding to the information and atmosphere of your story, and not clogging it up. As in so many things, it is often the case when using adjectives that less is more . . .

Adverb: Adverbs tell the reader how actions are performed – he ran 'slowly', she ate 'ravenously' – and, as such, they are an indispensable part of the writer's toolkit. But, as with adjectives, it's best to treat them cautiously. In fact, perhaps even more than adjectives. It's very easy to think that, once you've used an adverb, you've told the reader all they need to know, and, of course, in a way you have – but you've *told* them, rather than *shown* them, and you've not left them anything to imagine. So use adverbs sparingly, and only when you feel they're absolutely necessary. In fact, Stephen King, no mean slouch as an author, advocates never using adverbs at all, ever. Worth bearing in mind . . .

Antagonist: Otherwise known as the baddie, this is the villain against whom the hero or heroine has to struggle. Often nearly as clever, strong and formidable as the protagonist – but only nearly. An ingenious, worthwhile antagonist adds interest and spice to a story.

Compound sentence: A sentence with one or more subordinate clauses qualifying the main clause. Compound sentences are useful when slowly building up atmosphere, detail and character. Better avoided, though, when you want to build tension and pace as the connectives and subordinate clauses tend to slow things down.

First-person narrator: Put simply, this is where the protagonist is presented as being the teller of the tale. This is the technique used to enormous effect by Raymond Chandler in the Philip Marlowe books. It enables the writer to establish their protagonist's character in an extraordinarily intimate way, by revealing the unfolding events not just through the eyes, but also through the voice, of their protagonist. It is a technique that has both a strength and a weakness in the narrow viewpoint from which we see the action – the protagonist, and therefore the reader, can only know what they themselves see or learn about from being told by others. This can build the suspense very effectively but it can also hamper the flow of the story – you, as the writer, have to make sure that your protagonist can plausibly obtain all the information they need to solve the problem with which they're faced.

Lexicon: In this context, the range of vocabulary used by a character or the narrator of a story. It is all too easy, when writing, to give the narrator and all the characters the same voice – your voice. But the words each of us use are a sum of many things – upbringing, experience, education – and vary hugely depending on who we are talking to and what we want the outcome to be. A child in the playground learns early on that there is one lexicon that you use with your mates, and another when called into the head teacher's office. Using different lexicons in your writing is a subtle and effective way of providing information about your narrator and your characters to your reader.

Metaphor: A powerful and seductive tool in the writer's toolbox, and one to be used with judicious care. Metaphors are implied comparisons – 'the stench of failure', 'a sea of confusion', 'winged feet'. . . None of these refer to literal states; they draw on our associations with one thing, 'stench' for instance, to reinforce our understanding of the other. Metaphors can bring your writing to life and give it depth and texture. They can also slow it down, and, if the metaphors are particularly far-fetched and surprising to the reader, can stop your text dead in its tracks (metaphorically speaking).

Narrative present: Writing your story as if it is happening now – 'My hand gropes blindly for the alarm clock. My eyes open reluctantly. 2:30 a.m. – what was I thinking?' It has the advantage of immediacy, and of conveying the reader into the narrative with you, as if you were both experiencing it together, but it narrows the perspective, and makes it almost impossible to establish anything other than a single point of view. Effective if used with consciousness and care, though.

Omniscient narrator: The omniscient narrator is the most common narrative voice used in fiction writing and it comes with all sorts of benefits for the writer. Essentially, an omniscient narrator knows everything about everybody in the story, from their taste in coffee to their most intimate thoughts and feelings. Since all the characters are the writer's own creations, it is necessarily the case that the writer knows each inch of one of them. Equally, the fact that the writer shares that knowledge with the reader means that we, as readers, have a privileged view into the internal workings of a whole range of different people as they interact. We know each of them as well, or better, than we know ourselves. This is particularly powerful when the reader holds information about the thinking and motivation of different characters that they do not have about each other. When we know that the murderer is thinking about killing X, while we see X going blindly about their business of grocery shopping or cleaning out their closet, it gives a terrible feeling of powerless inevitability to the unfolding plot. The central drawback of an omniscient narrator is twofold. Firstly, it's very unlike life as we experience it – we have enough difficulty making out our own thoughts, intentions, emotions and motivations. Those of other people are at best guesswork. Secondly, it has to be handled very deftly, particularly in crime fiction, if suspense is to be maintained.

The solution to this is to use a tightly focused beam of omniscience, so to speak, where we, as readers, are privy to the innermost thoughts and feelings of the central character, but share that character's inability to see into the inner life of those they encounter – a bit like real life, in fact.

Past historic: The usual way of telling stories – it's something that's happened in the past, with the advantages of implying that a) the narrator knows what happened and b) there is an ending. Both of these make the reader feel pleasantly secure. Of course, you may not want your reader to feel secure, but creating a sense of anxiety and insecurity is best done deliberately, for effect. On the whole, kindness to your readers is rewarded with liking and loyalty, and is not something to dispense with lightly.

Plot: The plot is the series of events that occur in your story – the plot is made up, if you like, of the cogs and crankshafts and gears that make the story move along. But the plot is not the whole of the story, any more than the engine is the whole of a car.

Point of view: Also known in the scriptwriting trade as POV. When writing screenplays for TV or film, POV is given as an instruction to show from whose point of view the action is being seen – whose eyes the camera is looking through. The point of view is also crucial in fiction writing and can be conveyed in a number of ways. The most obvious is through the use of a first-person narrator so that the reader knows very clearly that we are seeing all the action from the point of view of X or Y or Z. This has its restrictions (see **First-person narrator**). The commonest device, so usual as to appear almost invisible to the reader, is to use third-person narrative – he, she – and an omniscient narrator (see **Omniscient narrator**). This enables the reader to get inside the head of the character through the observations and commentary provided by the narrator, such as 'Jane thought . . .', 'Michael felt . . .' It also enables the writer to move around easily from one character's point of view to another's so that the reader gets different perspectives on an event.

Protagonist: Sometimes, but not always, the hero or heroine, the protagonist is the main character around whom your story revolves, and in whom your reader has the greatest emotional investment and imaginative interest.

Showing: Presenting the elements in your story to the reader through metaphor, simile, imagery or dialogue, in such a way that they work out what is happening for themselves, rather than relying on what you have to tell them about it. Showing mimics the way in which we feel we apprehend experience in real life. As in almost everything to do with writing, there's a balancing act to be maintained between simply showing your reader what is happening and what it means, thereby making them do a substantial proportion of the interpretive work, and telling them (see **Telling**), which is more restful for the reader but also can come across as flat and controlling, as if you don't trust your reader to understand what is going on. It's very much your call, depending on the type of writing you're doing and the kind of relationship you want to build up with your reader.

Simile: A fancy name for a comparison, saying that something is 'like' or 'as' something else. An indispensable element in the writer's toolbox but, as with metaphors, to be used wisely and with a sense of how the simile is working in terms of the place, character, event or whatever you are describing. A good question to ask yourself is, 'How does this contribute to the reader's understanding of the story?' Everything you write has to work to that end.

Simple sentence: Very much as it sounds, a sentence with the bare minimum of parts to it – an article and a noun, possibly with an adjective, as the subject of a verb, possibly with an adverb, and another noun, again possibly with an adjective, as the object of the verb: 'The murderer cut off her fingers coldly.' This is a very effective sentence-form for fast-moving, action-packed scenes. You can't beat simple sentences for moving the action along and giving the reader a sense of breathlessness and excitement. It's a good idea to change pace every so often, though, and to use the occasional more complex sentence, simply to allow your reader time to rest and breathe a bit.

Story: The complete narrative, including all your plots, subplots, themes and imagery. The story is the totality of everything you have woven together to communicate your vision to your reader.

Subplot: A useful device to provide either contrast to or emphasis on your main plot. Subplots can develop minor characters who show the main characters in a new light, or pick up the main themes of your story and develop them in slightly different ways. They can be used to change pace – from high drama to light comedy, for instance – or to heighten the tension. The choice is yours. However you use them, sub-plots add texture and depth to the world you are creating.

Subordinate clause: Essentially, an additional piece of information about your main clause. In terms of how to use subordinate clauses when writing, it depends very much on the kind of world you are creating and the kind of pace at which you want your story to proceed. If you compare, for instance, the style of Chris Carter and that of Ben Aaronovitch from the passages quoted in this book (Chapters 6 and 11), you will see how the use of modifiers and subordinate clauses in Aaronovitch's writing provides a slow, layered, textured feel to the text, while Carter's spare, **simple sentences** move the action forward at speed.

Telling: Providing your reader with information directly, rather than allowing them to deduce it from imagery, dialogue, description and all the other tools in your toolbox. Telling is a necessary part of moving your story forward on occasions but needs to be balanced with showing if your story is not to become flat and uninteresting to the reader. Dickens, not a bad example to follow, always balanced showing and telling in his stories.

Theme: To some extent, you could say that the theme is what lies at the heart of the story – what the story is about when all the characters and events are stripped away. A lot of Dean Koontz's books, for instance, are concerned with themes of love, loss, loyalty and redemption. The plots may be different but the themes are usually the same. The theme is what you'd like to remain with your reader when the details of the plot have faded away. The less the themes are stated, but are implied through the action, the dialogue, the descriptions and the imagery, the more powerful they will be.

Third-person narrator: When the writer tells their story using the third person – 'he', 'she' and 'they'. Probably the commonest form of narrative, and certainly the most straightforward for the writer to deploy, not least because this is the usual format in which we tell our everyday stories of what happened at the office or in the sports club. The use of a third-person narrator immediately places the reader in a known and comfortable relationship to the storyteller – this is someone with something interesting to tell us. How much you, as the writer, build on or undermine that sense of comfort in the reader is entirely down to you and what you want your reader to feel. But a reliable third-person narrator is a very good baseline from which to start.

Unreliable narrator: The clue is in the title – the unreliable narrator is, in every sense of the word, a tricky character. One of the advantages of an omniscient narrator, from the reader's point of view, is that we can trust what they say – they provide the solid ground from which we view the unfolding action of the story. For instance, Jane Austen's narrators provide the reader with unquestionably the 'right' view from which to see the action. For good or ill, such a position of certainty is very rarely available in real life. The technique of the unreliable narrator is, in part, an answer to that problem, providing a viewpoint which is much more realistic in being partial and not necessarily accurate. It is not a technique much used in crime fiction, simply because of the critical importance of having a moral centre to the book, a vision of good and evil, on which the reader can rely. An interesting move in the direction of having an unreliable narrator as the protagonist of a crime novel is the figure of Jeff Lindsay's Dexter, the sympathetic serial killer. Lindsay neatly sidesteps the reader's uneasiness at sympathizing with a sociopath by locating the moral centre of the book in Harry's Code – the guidance provided by Dexter's foster father, Harry Morgan, to enable him to function as a serial killer, but only of supremely bad people.

USEFUL RESOURCES AND FURTHER READING

Conferences, courses and organizations

Theakstons Old Peculier Crime Writing Festival (www.oldpeculier crimefestival.co.uk): Europe's biggest crime-writing festival brings the best in crime fiction to Harrogate in a series of events, interviews and panel sessions over four days.

Crimefest (www.crimefest.com): Annual festival in Bristol drawing top crime novelists, editors, publishers, reviewers and readers from around the world in an informal atmosphere.

Bloody Scotland (www.bloodyscotland.com): Launched at the behest of successful Scottish crime writers such as Ian Rankin, Lin Anderson and Denise Mina, it features masterclasses and seminars with crime writers, theatrical events and dramatizations of crimes to be solved by participants.

Thriller School (http://thriller-school.com): An intensive annual crime-writing workshop in both Oxfordshire, UK, and California, USA. Talks from specialists in crime writing and crime fighting are accompanied by writing workshops throughout the weekend.

Crime Readers' Association (www.thecra.co.uk): News on crime writing and top authors, as well as tips and a major competition ('Debut Dagger') for new writers. Members receive a bi-weekly newsletter as well as a monthly magazine, *Crime Files*.

Magazines

Crime Fiction Fix (www.crimefictionfix.com): An online magazine for both readers and writers of crime fiction; includes access to a community of crime writers, as well as details of upcoming events in the UK and abroad.

Ellery Queen's Mystery Magazine (www.themysteryplace.com/eqmm): The world's most famous crime-fiction magazine is published in the US but offers international subscriptions; it promotes new crime writers through its 'Department of First Stories' section.

Websites

There is an ever-changing and vast array of resources online, offering information and contact details for crime-writing courses and communities, festivals and competitions, crime magazines, editorial consultancies and publishers. The most productive course of action is to be very clear about what you are looking for and search using appropriate keywords.

Works by highlighted authors

Ben Aaronovitch: *Broken Homes* (2013); *Whispers Under Ground* (2012); *Moon Over Soho* (2011); *Rivers of London* (2011).

Lin Anderson: *Picture Her Dead* (2011); *The Reborn* (2010); *Final Cut* (2009); *Easy Kill* (2008); *Dark Flight* (2007); *Blood Red Roses* (2005); *Deadly Code* (2005); *Torch* (2004); *Driftnet* (2003).

Truman Capote: *Summer Crossing* (posthumously published 2006); *Answered Prayers: The Unfinished Novel* (posthumously published 1986); *In Cold Blood* (1965); *Breakfast at Tiffany's* (1958); *The Grass Harp* (1951); *A Tree of Night and Other Stories* (1949); *Other Voices, Other Rooms* (1948).

Chris Carter: *One by One* (2013); *The Death Sculptor* (2012); *The Night Stalker* (2011); *The Executioner* (2010); *The Crucifix Killer* (2009).

Lee Child: *Never Go Back* (2013); *A Wanted Man* (2012); *The Affair* (2011); *Worth Dying For* (2010); *61 Hours* (2010); *Gone Tomorrow* (2009); *Nothing to Lose* (2008); *Bad Luck and Trouble* (2007); *The Hard Way* (2006); *One Shot* (2005); *The Enemy* (2004); *Persuader* (2003); *Without Fail* (2002); *Echo Burning* (2001); *Running Blind* (US)/*The Visitor* (UK) (2000); *Tripwire* (1999); *Die Trying* (1998); *Killing Floor* (1997).

Michael Connelly: *The Gods of Guilt* (2013); *The Black Box* (2012); *The Drop* (2011); *The Fifth Witness* (2011); *The Reversal* (2010); *Nine Dragons* (2009); *The Scarecrow* (2009); *The Brass Verdict* (2008); *The Overlook* (2007); *Echo Park* (2006); *The Lincoln Lawyer* (2005); *The Closers* (2005); *The Narrows* (2004); *Lost Light* (2003); *Chasing the Dime* (2002); *City of Bones* (2002); *A Darkness More than Night* (2001); *Void Moon* (2000); *Angels Flight* (1999); *Blood Work* (1998); *Trunk Music* (1997); *The Poet* (1996); *The Last Coyote* (1995); *The Concrete Blonde* (1994); *The Black Ice* (1993); *The Black Echo* (1992).

Patricia Cornwell: *Dust* (2013); *The Bone Bed* (2012); *Red Mist* (2011); *Port Mortuary* (2010); *The Scarpetta Factor* (2009); *The Front* (2008); *Scarpetta* (2008); *Book of the Dead* (2007); *At Risk* (2006); *Predator* (2005); *Trace* (2004);

Blow Fly (2003); *Isle of Dogs* (2001); *The Last Precinct* (2000); *Black Notice* (1999); *Southern Cross* (1999); *Point of Origin* (1998); *Unnatural Exposure* (1997); *Hornet's Nest* (1997); *Cause of Death* (1996); *From Potter's Field* (1995); *The Body Farm* (1994); *Cruel and Unusual* (1993); *All That Remains* (1992); *Body of Evidence* (1991); *Postmortem* (1990).

Charles Cumming: *A Foreign Country* (2012); *The Trinity Six* (2011); *Typhoon* (2008); *The Spanish Game* (2006); *The Hidden Man* (2003); *A Spy by Nature* (2001).

Lindsey Davis: *A Cruel Fate* (2014); *Enemies at Home* (2014); *Master of God* (2012); *Nemesis* (2010); *Alexandria* (2009); *Rebels and Traitors* (2009); *Saturnalia* (2007); *See Delphi and Die* (2005); *Scandal Takes a Holiday* (2004); *The Accusers* (2003); *The Jupiter Myth* (2002); *A Body in the Bath House* (2001); *Ode to a Banker* (2000); *One Virgin Too Many* (1999); *Two for the Lions* (1998); *Three Hands in the Fountain* (1997); *A Dying Light in Corduba* (1996); *Time to Depart* (1995); *Last Act in Palmyra* (1994); *Poseidon's Gold* (1993); *The Iron Hand of Mars* (1992); *Venus in Copper* (1991); *Shadows in Bronze* (1990); *The Silver Pigs* (1989).

Jeffrey Deaver: *Trouble in Mind* (2014); *The Skin Collector* (2014); *The October List* (2013); *The Kill Room* (2013); *XO: A Kathryn Dance Thriller* (2012); *Carte Blanche: A James Bond Novel* (2011); *Edge* (2010); *The Burning Wire* (2010); *Roadside Crosses* (2009); *The Bodies Left Behind* (2008); *The Broken Window* (2008); *The Sleeping Doll* (2007); *The Cold Moon* (2006); *The Twelfth Card* (2005); *Garden of Beasts* (2004); *The Vanished Man* (2003); *The Stone Monkey* (2002); *The Blue Nowhere* (2001); *Hell's Kitchen* (2001); *Speaking in Tongues* (2000); *The Empty Chair* (2000); *The Devil's Teardrop* (1999); *The Coffin Dancer* (1998); *The Bone Collector* (1997); *A Maiden's Grave* (1995); *Praying for Sleep* (1994); *The Lesson of Her Death* (1993); *Bloody River Blues* (1993); *Mistress of Justice* (1992); *Shallow Graves* (1992); *Hard News* (1991); *Death of a Blue Movie Star* (1990); *Manhattan Is My Beat* (1988).

David Hewson: *The House of Dolls* (2014); *The Killing III* (2014); *The Killing II* (2013); *The Killing* (2012); *Macbeth* (with A. J. Hartley) (2012); *Judith and the Holy Fearns* (2011); *Carnival for the Dead* (2011); *The Fallen Angel* (2011); *The Blue Deacon* (aka *City of Fear*) (2010); *Dead Man's Socks* (2010); *The Garden of Evil* (2008); *Dante's Numbers* (aka *The Dante Killings*) (2008); *The Sacred Sacrament* (2007); *The Promised Land* (2007); *The Lizard's Bite* (2006); *The Sacred Cut* (2005); *The Villa of Mysteries* (2004); *A Season for the Dead* (2003); *Lucifer's Shadow* (aka *The Cemetery of Secrets*) (2001); *Native Rites* (2000); *Solstice* (1998); *Semana Santa* (aka *Death in Seville*) (1996); *Epiphany* (1996).

Donna Leon: *Drawing Conclusions* (2011); *A Question of Belief* (2010); *About Face* (2009); *The Girl of His Dreams* (2008); *Suffer the Little Children* (2007); *Through a Glass, Darkly* (2006); *Blood from a Stone* (2005); *Doctored Evidence* (2004); *Uniform Justice* (2003); *Wilful Behaviour* (2002); *A Sea of Troubles* (2001); *Friends in High Places* (2000); *Fatal Remedies* (1999); *A Noble Radiance* (1998); *The Death of Faith* (aka *Quietly in Their Sleep*) (1997); *Acqua Alta* (1996); *Death and Judgment* (aka *A Venetian Reckoning*) (1994); *Dressed for Death* (aka *The Anonymous Venetian*) (1994); *Death in a Strange Country* (1993); *Death at La Fenice* (1992).

Ian Rankin: *Saints of the Shadow Bible* (2013); *Standing in Another Man's Grave* (2012); *The Impossible Dead* (2011); *A Cool Head* (2009); *The Complaints* (2009); *Dark Entries* (2009); *Doors Open* (2008); *Exit Music* (2007); *The Naming of the Dead* (2006); *Fleshmarket Close* (2004); *A Question of Blood* (2003); *Resurrection Men* (2002); *The Falls* (2001); *Set in Darkness* (2000); *Dead Souls* (1999); *The Hanging Garden* (1998); *Black & Blue* (1997); *Let It Bleed* (1995); *Blood Hunt* (1995); *Mortal Causes* (1994); *Bleeding Hearts* (1994); *The Black Book* (1993); *Witch Hunt* (1993); *Strip Jack* (1992); *Tooth & Nail* (1992); *Hide & Seek* (1991); *Westwind* (1990); *Watchman* (1988); *Knots & Crosses* (1987); *The Flood* (1986).

Nicola Slade: *Scuba Dancing* (2005); *Murder Most Welcome* (2008); *Death Is the Cure* (2009); *Murder Fortissimo* (2011); *Crowded Coffin* (2013); *The Dead Queen's Garden* (2013).

David Smith: *Evil Relations* (aka *Witness*) (2011).

INDEX